757
SEATTLE'S ROCKET

I f you're familiar with Boeing's range of airliners you're certain to know the Boeing 757, and if you've taken an intra-continental flight in recent years, you've probably flown on the type.

Since the 757 made its first flight on February 19, 1982, Boeing's production facility at Renton, Washington built 1,050 aircraft.

The 757 and the 767 broke Boeing's design mould. Both types differed considerably from the framer's 707, 737 and 727. The original triad were all configured with similar looking forward fuselages, vertical stabilisers, and wing sweeps. Wing sweep and vertical stabiliser aside, the most noticeable differences of the 757 is the forward fuselage configuration and the aircraft's height above the ramp.

Unlike the 737 and 777, the 757 is not a multi-generation type with just two baseline models put into production: the original 757-200 and the slightly longer 757-300, of which just 55 were built.

Today, a couple of 757 operators are notable: Delta Air Lines, the biggest carrier in the world based at Atlanta, Georgia and DHL which operates its freighter fleet painted in a vivid all-yellow colour scheme, from its headquarters at Bonn, Germany.

Delta Air Lines is a North American scheduled carrier and DHL is a European logistics company with a large air freight division. Both have a significant share in their respective markets

Given its seating capacity, suitability to inter-city routes, a low operating cost base, and that it is a very effective freighter, operators like the 757.

But the 757 is not just a commercial jet. Government leaders and chiefs of staff also fly on military variants of the 757 in the specialised VIP air transportation role and the more straightforward cargo airlift tasking.

Whatever your interest in aviation, Boeing 757: Seattle's Rocket is packed full of features about different variants, including extensive content on the freighters, flying testbeds, and the US Air Force C-32 painted in a stylish blue-and-white livery, used to transport the President and other government leaders.

Mark Ayton
Editor

Contents

MAIN COVER IMAGE: DAVE STURGES/AIRTEAM IMAGES

AIRTEAMIMAGES/ENA MONMORADO

NASA

70

AIRTEAMIMAGES/EUROPIX

28

ISBN: 978 1 83632 133 0
Editor: Mark Ayton
Revisions/updates: Paul Hamblin
Senior editor, specials: Roger Mortimer
Email: roger.mortimer@keypublishing.com
Cover Design: Steve Donovan
Design: SJmagic DESIGN SERVICES, India
Advertising Sales Manager: Sam Clark
Email: sam.clark@keypublishing.com
Tel: 01780 755131
Advertising Production: Becky Antoniades
Email: Rebecca.antoniades@keypublishing.com

SUBSCRIPTION/MAIL ORDER
Key Publishing Ltd, PO Box 300, Stamford, Lincs, PE9 1NA
Tel: 01780 480404
Subscriptions email: subs@keypublishing.com

Mail Order email: orders@keypublishing.com
Website: www.keypublishing.com/shop

PUBLISHING
Group CEO: Adrian Cox
Publisher: Steve O'Hara

Published by
Key Publishing Ltd, PO Box 100, Stamford, Lincs, PE9 1XQ
Tel: 01780 755131 **Website:** www.keypublishing.com

PRINTING
Precision Colour Printing Ltd, Haldane,
Halesfield 1, Telford, Shropshire. TF7 4QQ

DISTRIBUTION
Seymour Distribution Ltd, 2 Poultry Avenue, London,
EC1A 9PU
Enquiries Line: 02074 294000.

Introducing
The Boeing 757

Barry Lloyd introduces the Boeing 757, renowned for high performance and good economics, and later life service as freighters.

The success of the 727 was undoubtedly highly satisfactory for Boeing's management in Seattle with more than 1,800 being built, and in the mid-1970s, an era of high demand for new aircraft, the manufacturer studied a stretched and modified version, to be known as the 727-300. However, following discussions with existing operators, this was quickly discarded in favour of a completely new design, called the 7N7, which would reflect, among other things, the recent advances in construction techniques together with improved high-bypass turbofan engines.

Development began at Boeing's Renton, Washington State factory in March 1979. The 7N7, soon renamed 757, was designed to be more capable and more efficient than the 727. The original plans called for a fuselage similar in length to the 727, but having looked at the initial drawings, the designers decided to build the first series with a longer fuselage, so there was never a -100 version as such. The twin-engine configuration was chosen for greater fuel efficiency versus its predecessors and with a proposed length of 155ft 4in (47.3m), the 757-200 would be 2ft 1in (640mm) longer »

Monarch Airlines operated a fleet of ten 757-200s until the carrier ceased operations in October 2017. G-MONK is seen at Skiathos, Greece.
AIRTEAMIMAGES/TIMO BREIDENSTEIN

than the 727-200, but with a completely redesigned interior, thus allowing a greater amount of cabin space. Of all the Boeing 757s built, the vast majority, almost 1,000, were 757-200s. The interior would typically offer seating for 239 passengers, 50 more than its predecessor.

Operating costs were at the forefront of the design targets, principally because of rapidly increasing fuel costs following the 1973 Arab Israeli War. Lighter materials were incorporated, together with redesigned wings. The 757s high thrust-to-weight ratio allowed take-offs from shorter runways and airfields with hot and high conditions. Computer-aided design, originally conceived for the 767, was used for more than one-third of the 757's design drawings.

New Line

Boeing built a special assembly line at its Renton factory to produce the 757. Both British Airways and Rolls-Royce lobbied on behalf of the British aircraft industry to manufacture 757 wings at an early stage in the development programme, but Boeing was determined to produce at least half of the aircraft's components themselves, including the wings, empennage, and nose section. The remaining assembly parts were subcontracted to primarily US-based companies. As the 727 programme was being wound down, the 757 began to take over. The production aircraft was 3,600lb (1,630kg) lighter than originally specified. As a result of this, it recorded a rate of fuel burn 3% better than expected, which resulted in a useful range increase of 200nm (370km).

Initial orders came from British Airways and Eastern Airlines. Both carriers chose the Rolls-Royce RB-211-535C powerplant. This marked the first time that a Boeing airliner had been launched with engines produced outside the US. Pratt & Whitney offered the PW 2037 turbofan, which Delta Air Lines adopted. A version of the General Electric CF6-32 engine was also marketed, but there was insufficient demand, and the project was abandoned.

A Slow Success

The prototype, N757A, was rolled out on January 13, 1982, with the first flight taking place on February 19 and its FAA certification achieved on December 21. The first customer delivery was to Eastern Airlines the following day and the carrier lost no time in placing the aircraft into revenue service, which began on January 1, 1983.

Despite the launch orders, the aircraft was not an instant success, even though no direct competitor existed at the time. By then, fuel prices were quite stable, which encouraged many operators to stay with their 727 and DC-9/MD-80 derivatives. Smaller aircraft were being favoured because of the increased competition brought about by the changes in the market, following deregulation in the United States.

In the late 1980s, with fuel prices escalating again and their existing fleets beginning to age, the major US carriers began to take a second look at the type and orders started to build

up. It was not until the late 1980s that orders per year were around 100, as carriers in other parts of the world began to realise the potential of the 757, and as a result it was soon wearing many different colour schemes.

Good Performance

To those handling the 757 on the ground, the first impression is one of size. It can give the illusion of being a widebody, sitting as it does much higher than comparable aircraft on its tall undercarriage. This design feature was needed to accommodate the powerplants, which also appear to be bigger than necessary. However, the thrust they provide gives the aircraft a power-to-weight ratio exceeded only by Concorde, and pilots often refer to its sports car performance.

The 757 can be off the runway in 4,000ft (1,220m), with a rotation speed of 140kts (259kph). After take-off it can comfortably climb direct to its cruising altitude. In comparison, a 737 requires a step climb procedure requiring the aircraft to climb to a given altitude and level off where it can burn off more fuel to lighten the load enabling it to climb to the desired flight level.

One side effect of the 757's design was only discovered after it entered service. Wake turbulence, the air disturbance caused by the progress of an aircraft through the sky, has no effect on the aircraft itself but can cause significant problems for any aircraft following in its wake. In fact, early versions of the 757 caused more wake turbulence than a 747. Following two fatal crashes involving General Aviation types and reports that smaller airliners had been affected, FAA investigators began to study the 757's wake turbulence characteristics. Its aft-loaded wing design was thought to be the culprit, although the actual cause was never conclusively established. The later addition of winglets, originally designed to improve performance and fuel burn, unintentionally reduced wake turbulence, but because of the inherent problem, FAA air traffic control regulations were amended to require greater separation behind the 757 than other large-category jets. For this reason, the 757 became the only airliner in its category to be classed as heavy.

Variants

At the Farnborough Airshow in September 1996, Boeing announced a launch order from German charter carrier Condor for 12 of the stretched 757-300. This incorporated a 23ft 5in (7.13m) stretch compared with the 757-200, resulting in room for 50 more passengers, making it the longest single-aisle twinjet ever built. Rolls-Royce and Pratt & Whitney were able to supply uprated 535-24 and PW 2040 powerplants respectively for the extended version. The first of these was rolled out on May 31, 1998 and completed its maiden flight on August 2 that year. The initial example entered service with Condor on March 19, 1999. Additional orders for the 757-300 were placed by several US carriers, namely American Trans Air, Continental Airlines and Northwest Airlines. Attempts to sell it to American Airlines and United Airlines were unsuccessful, primarily because of their financial status at the time. The premise offered by Boeing was an alternative for the 767-200. Icelandair and Arkia Israeli Airlines took the extended version, but few of the other big European charter companies selected it. Concerned by falling sales, Boeing began a review of the production rates for the 757.

Despite being designed for short to medium routes, some operators were quick to realise that the 757 had a hidden talent. In 1986, the FAA approved RB211-powered 757s for ETOPS (Extended-range Twin-engine Operational Performance Standards), a set of safety regulations governing twinjet flights over remote regions or expanses of water, such as the North ❯❯

Atlantic. Approval for the PW 2040 followed later. Regulators based their decision on their reliable performance record on extended transcontinental US services while also considering precedents set by the 767. With the introduction of ETOPS, flights of 4,000 miles (6,437km) from Western Europe to the US East Coast were easily achievable.

First Operations

Eastern Airlines initially put the aircraft on the Atlanta-Tampa route, while British Airways began using it on its London-Belfast shuttle services on February 9, 1983, replacing the Trident 3 in the process. Among other early operators were UK-based holiday charter carriers Monarch Airlines and Air Europe, who began 757 operations later that year. The biggest orders came from the US carriers, with Northwest Airlines placing an order for 20 aircraft in November 1983.

The hub-and-spoke concept, first introduced in the US in the early 1980s, brought increasing congestion at the hub airports and this, coupled with new noise

Spanish flag carrier Iberia swelled its fleet with 30 757-200s, the last of which was relinquished in late 2008. EC-HDV (c/n 26254) is seen at Amsterdam Airport Schiphol.
AIRTEAMIMAGES/OLIVIER CORNELOUP

regulations, made carriers begin to look at ways of overcoming these constraints. One solution was the 757 with its larger capacity and quieter engines. Between 1988 and 1989 American and United placed combined orders for 160, with that figure being doubled by carriers elsewhere in the world.

The 757 was becoming a common sight on the US route networks, spurred on by its ability to operate out of noise-restricted airports such as John Wayne-Orange County, California, and Washington National, as it was then known. Delta and American Airlines would ultimately operate fleets of more than 100 aircraft each. If there was any downside to the 757 operation, it was simply that loading and unloading a single-aisle aircraft of this size took longer than for previous models, but this was largely cancelled out by the improved route performance.

Among the European scheduled carriers Iberia opted for 30 aircraft and Icelandair (which currently has 11 examples) were notable customers. Further afield in Asia, a demonstration tour in 1982 was unable to bring much in the way of orders. Japan Air Lines was a potential early customer, but ultimately decided against ordering the type. Singapore Airlines (SIA) placed an order for four aircraft, which were delivered in 1984, but they only saw five years' service with the airline before

being sold to American Trans Air, with SIA preferring the A310. In China there was more interest, where various carriers found the 757 useful for their medium and longer domestic routes.

The 757 was proving to be a winner in many operational areas. Airlines were impressed by the lower fuel burn and the greater payload capability compared with its predecessors. The need for a flight engineer had also been eliminated, helped by the introduction of cathode ray tube (CRT) instrumentation, a significant innovation at the time.

US Fleets

It would come as no surprise to Boeing that the biggest operators of the 757 were in the United States. The largest fleet was with American Airlines (AA), which operated 177, all 757-200 series, most of them being delivered new from the manufacturer, but some were acquired through buy-outs of existing airlines. This meant that the powerplants were a mixture of both the Rolls-Royce RB211 and in the case of the former TWA aircraft, the PW 2037. Prior to the COVID-19 pandemic, American Airlines planned to dispose of its entire fleet by the end of 2021, but this was accelerated by a year. Some aircraft, following conversion, have been taken up by the cargo market and others with passenger carriers, but the majority were scrapped or stored.

Of the United States' legacy carriers, only Delta operated the 757-300, 16 of which were acquired following its takeover of Northwest in 2008; these were normally scheduled on the high-density routes, such as those to Hawaii and from Minneapolis to Seattle and Los Angeles. Its 757-300s were configured with 234 seats: 24 in first class, 32 in Premium Economy, known as Delta Comfort+, and 178 in economy class. Additionally, Delta had 111 757-200s, a typical configuration for which would be 187 seats, 16 first class and 171 in coach, though this varied according to the routes on which they were being flown. In recognition of their service to the airline, one example, N608DA, is on display at the Delta Flight Museum in Atlanta.

United Airlines was the second biggest operator of the type, also with a mixed 757-200 and 757-300 fleet, 51 being 757-200s and 21 757-300s from the takeover of Continental Airlines. Configurations varied, depending on whether the aircraft were being used on domestic or transatlantic routes, with a business class of 16-28 seats, » together with a range of between 114 and 160 seats offered in coach (economy).

European Charter Operators

In Europe, both the 757-200 and 757-300 proved popular for use on the inclusive tour routes from northern Europe to the Mediterranean and beyond. Generally, few carriers offered any class of seat other than economy, Condor of Germany being the exception with a small premium economy section of 26 seats, and 236 in economy. Prior to its demise, Thomas Cook was able to offer 280 seats in its 757-300 models. Several other European charter airlines, including Air 2000, Air Holland, and LTU International, were also customers for the twinjet in the late 1980s.

In contrast, an attempt was made by a French airline, La Compagnie, to open a scheduled service between London's Luton and New York's Newark International airport with just 74 seats, which can be converted to flat beds, on its two 757-200s. The service was short-lived, beginning in March 2015 and ending in September of the following year. However, La Compagnie has continued to operate the service from Paris Orly to New York/Newark.

Ethiopian Airlines flew a mixed fleet of 12 aircraft, all 757-200s, five of which were new and the remainder either leased or acquired from the second-hand market. Of these, two were freighters, two were PF (combi) aircraft and the remainder were fitted in an all-passenger configuration. Of those, two were equipped to operate in the ER (extended range) configuration.

Production of the 757 came to an end in October 2004, with 1,050 aircraft having gone down the line. The final delivery was B-2866 (c/n 34009) to Xiamen Airlines in China on April 27, 2005. The question for the existing operators was: 'How do we replace it?'

Those wanting to buy a more updated version of the 757 were offered the larger 737NG versions, the 737-800 and 900 series, as potential successors, and later the 737 MAX, but the problems with the MAX, well documented as they were, meant operators were reluctant to place orders. Boeing has said it is looking at a 757 successor, which it initially explored with Embraer under the title NMA or New Mid-sized Aircraft,

however, the failure to tie up a deal with the Brazilian framer caused Boeing to completely reconsider the situation. A suitable 757 replacement would require a greater range and more seats than the existing model to compete with the success of the Airbus A321.

A New Life Without Passengers

Since the early part of the 21st century, the continual growth of package and general courier services has caused massive demand for freighter aircraft. Many of the legacy carriers have had cargo-only jets in their fleets for many years, which have largely dealt with the cargo and mail demand that coincided with their own route networks. The exponential growth of online ordering, plus a year-round demand for fresh produce from all over the globe, has meant that all-cargo operators have grown significantly. FedEx, UPS, and DHL are probably the best known. Less well known is China's SF Airlines.

All these aircraft began their lives carrying passengers and have been converted into full cargo versions from their previous role, with almost all sourced from other operators.

The COVID-19 outbreak had a significant positive effect on the cargo business. The huge demand for medical equipment of all kinds, coupled with the ever-expanding need for all-cargo services saw the 757 operating all over the world. Most examples were fitted with a glass cockpit and this, together with the installation of winglets, made it a favourite with pilots and management alike.

Manchester-based Thomas Cook Airlines, a charter operator, was founded from the merger of Thomas Cook Group and MyTravel Group. Flight service ended in September 2019 following compulsory liquidation. The carrier operated two dozen 757-200s.
AIRTEAMIMAGES/MATTHIEU DOUHAIRE

Billion Dollar
GAMBLE

Mark Ayton reviews the development of the Boeing 757 and examines the basis for the framer's decision to launch.

Boeing's decision to launch the 757 in March 1979 has its roots in two very different aircraft: the framer's own 727 trijet and Concorde. The American aerospace industry caught the jitters about the Anglo-French development of the supersonic Concorde airliner.

American aerospace thinking was so off the wall at the time that its leaders thought that once fully developed, Concorde would be the only long-range passenger jet that the world's airlines would want. How wrong those leaders were, despite its elegance and stunning performance, only 14 production

standard Concordes were ever built, making the jet one of the least commercially viable aircraft ever for all kinds of reasons which remain outside the scope of this feature. Because of Concorde's development, the Americans feared being left behind in the commercial supersonic passenger jet market such that the US Congress funded a competition for the design and production of America's first supersonic airliner. President Kennedy had committed the US government to subsidise the programme.

America's Supersonic Transport

Launched in June 1963, Boeing, Lockheed, and North American all responded to the government's request with just Boeing's 2707 and Lockheed's L-2000 selected. Their task was to design and produce a bigger, faster, and longer-range supersonic aircraft compared to Concorde. Boeing won with its 250-passenger swing-wing Model 2707 which eventually switched to a delta wing design due to weight gain. However, programme funding was cancelled by the US government in March 1971 because of sonic boom noise concerns and rising costs.

Boeing then pursued development of the 7X7, a short-haul aircraft with quiet operating credentials until the oil crisis struck in 1973, largely because of the Yom Kippur War and resulting fuel price increases. Consequently, Boeing's design emphasis switched to greater fuel efficiency versus noise reduction.

The framer stuck with the 7X7 designation, but its development engineers shifted to wide-body designs and 12-months on, an aircraft with a single-aisle configuration emerged from Boeing's Seattle den.

It was a stretched 727, dubbed the 727-300 to feature an 18ft (5m) longer fuselage, strengthened landing gears, more efficient wings, more powerful Pratt & Whitney JT8D-217 engines, lighter materials, and showcased recent advances in manufacturing techniques.

Early research findings proved positive – the production aircraft was 3,600lb lighter than originally specified and, as a result, it achieved a fuel burn rate that was 3% better than expected, resulting in a range increase of 200nm.

Boeing had earmarked United Airlines as the 727-300's launch customer, but United Airlines did not buy in to the programme, reportedly

because its fuel efficiency was not sufficient.

Boeing struggled on with its plan to develop the wide-body 7X7 and a single-aisle design dubbed in January 1976 as the 7N7. The two proposed aircraft were subsequently launched as the Boeing 767 and the Boeing 757 respectively.

Initial 7N7 proposals called for a fuselage similar in length to the 727, but having looked at the preliminary drawings, engineers decided to build the first series with a longer fuselage designated the 757-200, as such, there was never a 757-100 version.

A twin-engine approach was selected due to the greater fuel economy, immediately separating it from its trijet predecessor. With a proposed length of 155ft 4in, the 757-200 would be 2ft 1in longer than the 727-200, but with a completely redesigned cabin. Boeing designers intended the new jet to typically seat 239 passengers – some 50 more than the 727 – despite retaining the single aisle configuration.

Just like the 727-300, Boeing had a launch customer earmarked for its new 757: Miami-based Eastern Air Lines. But the Seattle-centric framer was also hopeful that the United Kingdom would play a big part in　》

Eastern Airlines 757-200 N519EA (c/n 22209) was delivered to the carrier in November 1984 and withdrawn from use in early 1991. The jet went on to serve with Birgenair, America West and US Airways before being scrapped.
AIRTEAMIMAGES/WORLD AVIATION ARCHIVE

the launch of the 757 thanks to the involvement of flag carrier British Airways (with a 757 order), engine manufacturer Rolls-Royce (supply of engines), and aircraft manufacturer British Aerospace (production of the wings under a partnership).

Once estimates were submitted to Boeing by British Aerospace for wing production, their 757 managers must have fallen off their chairs from the shock caused by the high costs presented to them by the Brits. Not

DHL Boeing 757-200F G-BIKF (c/n 22177) during loading at Warsaw-Chopin Airport. AIRTEAMIMAGES/ JAN OSTROWSKI

for the first time, the UK's aerospace manufacturing cost base crippled the chance of the British company making wings for the 757. With hindsight it was not a bad situation. British Aerospace went on to partner in the Airbus consortium making wings, a manufacturing activity that continues today at the Airbus UK facility at Broughton, North Wales.

The other two UK companies, British Airways and Rolls-Royce did participate in the 757 programme with details

of the type's launch orders (British Airways and Eastern each ordered 20 aircraft, all powered by Rolls-Royce RB211 engines) announced on August 31, 1978.

This marked the first time that a Boeing civilian airliner had been launched with engines produced outside the United States. Pratt & Whitney offered the PW2037 turbofan, which Delta Air Lines later adopted. A version of the General Electric CF6-32 was also promoted, but there was insufficient commercial demand, and the option was eventually abandoned.

Boeing's announcement was the public side of the 757's launch, within the Boeing's Seattle den, programme managers, engineers, and production specialists were faced with recruiting employees, selecting subcontractors, design and manufacturing tooling and the parts (47% of the 95,000 different parts were computer-designed), compiling and writing assembly documents, not to mention winning additional sales to inject much needed funding into the programme.

Computer-aided design, originally conceived for the 767, was used for more than one-third of the 757's project drawings. While snubbed by many today as little more than a stretched narrowbody, the 757 pushed the envelope in many areas of how a modern airliner could and should be conceptualised.

This massive effort led to Boeing signing contracts with subcontractors worth a record-breaking $1bn for 757 fuselage sections on October 11, 1979. What was different about these contract awards was the basis upon which they were awarded, using approximate cost estimates as opposed to the usual detailed estimates.

Assembly and Certification

The 757-assembly line at Renton was purpose-built comprising six stations, with an individual aircraft moved from station to station to complete all six assembly events ready for roll-out.

Assembly started with each wing mated to the respective side of the mid-fuselage section, levelled within its tooling by hydraulic jacks. This was followed by mating of the aft fuselage section with neither the vertical nor horizontal stabilisers fitted. The forward fuselage section was the last to be mated, hoisted in place to align with the two wing sections.

Major 757 components were made at locations away from the Renton final assembly line. Boeing facilities manufactured the empennage, forward fuselage, and wings while subcontractors manufactured others; Fairchild Aircraft (leading edge slats), Grumman (flaps) and Rockwell International (centre fuselage section).

Boeing started an 11-month flight-test programme using the first five 757 aircraft built, each tasked with separate tests. It was originally planned to involve 1,254 hours.

Into Service

Boeing 757 prototype, registered N757A (c/n 22212), was rolled out »

Boeing 757 Test Aircraft				
Line number	c/n	Registration	First operator	Delivery date to first operator
1	22212	N757A	Boeing Airplane Company	February 1982
2	22191	N501EA	Eastern Air Lines	August 1983
3	22192	N502EA	Eastern Air Lines	September 1983
4	22193	N503EA	Eastern Air Lines	May 1983
5	22194	N504EA	Eastern Air Lines	February 1983

Boeing 757 Facts

Until Airbus and Boeing introduced their respective A320 Family and 737 models to the market powered by new, efficient engines, the following facts were held by the Boeing 757.

- Pilots rated the 757's short-field performance as good thanks to its large, efficient wing with slats, double-slotted flaps, and optional winglets.
- The 757-200 had the highest thrust-to-weight ratio of any airliner except Concorde at 240,000lb take-off weight and 77,000 to 80,000lb of thrust generated by either Pratt & Whitney PW2037s or Rolls-Royce RB211-535E4 turbofans. With a full load of passengers and cargo, a 757-200 can fly a straight climb to 35,000ft from a 7,000ft long runway with a flight range of 2,000nm.
- Pilots rated the 757's flight deck as spacious and comfortable thanks to the blunt, low-slung nose, and the maximum fuselage diameter maintained so far forward.
- Given its larger size compared to other narrow body jets, the 757 offers greater range and cheaper operating costs than a wide-body aircraft.
- Pilot's rated the 757's controllability as neither light nor heavy with neither a rapid or delayed response rate from a control input, with perfectly coupled pitch, roll, and yaw.
- For operators, the 757 is profitable on both short-haul domestic and trans-Atlantic routes.

on January 13, 1982, with the maiden sortie taking place on February 19. Certification by the US Federal Aviation Administration (FAA) followed on December 21, with the first customer delivery to Eastern Air Lines the following day. Keen to start the new year on a high, Eastern Air Lines wasted no time in putting its new flagship to work when the inaugural revenue service of the 757 took place on January 1, 1983. The following month, British Airways started using the 757 for its London to Belfast link, where

it replaced the flag carrier's Hawker Siddeley Trident 3Bs.

Initial customers of the type confirmed its improved dispatch reliability and quieter performance compared with previous-generation jets. Airlines reported lower operating costs born out of improved fuel burn and the use of a two-crew cockpit. Compared with the 707 and 727, the twinjet burnt 42% and 40% less fuel per seat, respectively. If there was any downside to 757 operations, it was simply that loading and unloading a single-aisle aircraft of this size took longer than previous-generation models, but this was largely cancelled out by improved route performance.

Despite a flurry of launch orders and impressive operating economics, the new narrowbody was not the instant success Boeing had hoped for.

Even though no direct competitor existed for the 757, the relative stability of fuel prices at the time of its launch and the wider macroeconomic environment convinced many potential buyers to stick with their existing examples – resulting in a somewhat stagnating orderbook.

Aviation is perhaps one of the most cyclical industries, with countless external factors influencing the ebb and flow of demand. Sure enough, by the late 1980s, fuel prices were on the rise once again and carriers　　　》

Boeing 757-200 N521AT (c/n 24368) on lease to Air Berlin from American Trans Air seen at Dusseldorf Airport. AIRTEAMIMAGES/ WOLFGANG MENDORF

Boeing 757 Timeline

Date	Event
January 13, 1982	Boeing rolled-out the first ever Boeing 757 (N757A, c/n 22212), a 757-200 model, at its Renton, Washington facility.
February 17, 1982	Boeing rolled the aircraft under its own power for the first time at Renton Municipal Airport for taxi tests.
February 19, 1982	Boeing conducted the maiden flight of the 757 from Renton Municipal Airport. The aircraft's take-off weight was 185,000lb, its rotation speed was 125kts, and lift-off required 3,700ft. The aircraft landed at Paine Field, Everett home of the Boeing 747 and 767 production facilities after the 2-hour, 31-minute flight. The flight started the 11-month flight-test programme.
December 22, 1982	Eastern Airlines received its first two Boeing 757s, N506EA (c/n 22196) and N507EA (c/n 22197).
January 1, 1983	The 757 entered service with Eastern Airlines.
February 9, 1983	The 757 entered service with British Airways. The 757 initially operated shuttle services on UK domestic routes followed by major trunk destinations in mainland Europe.
December 1983	Boeing rolled out the first Pratt & Whitney powered 757. Delta Air Lines received the first of two jets on November 5, 1984. N602DL (c/n 22809) and N603DL (c/n 22810).
1986	Rolls-Royce powered 757s received ETOPS certification.
1992	Pratt & Whitney powered 757s received ETOPS certification.
September 1996	Boeing launched the Boeing 757-300.
April 10, 1997	Boeing engineers completed a key milestone in the design of the 757-300 on April 1, 1997, when engineers released 25% of all design drawings for the aircraft. Completion of the drawings meant Boeing factories and suppliers could begin fabrication of aircraft parts assemblies, and machine tools.
February 3, 1998	Boeing rolled out the first forward fuselage section for the new Boeing 757-300 at its Wichita, Kansas facility where it was manufactured.
May 31, 1998	Boeing introduced its newest aircraft, the 757-300 (N757X, c/n 29016), at a roll out celebration at the company's Renton manufacturing facility.
August 2, 1998	The first Boeing 757-300 (N757X, c/n 29016) made the type's maiden flight taking off from Renton Municipal Airport at 10:08 PDT painted in Boeing's red, white, and blue livery. The jet was flown by Boeing test pilots Leon Robert and Jerry Whites throughout the 2-hour 25-minute flight.
January 27, 1999	The Boeing 757-300 received concurrent FAA and JAA type certification after passing the flight-testing and certification processes. To obtain certification, Boeing used three 757-300s to conduct a 5.5-month flight-test programme. Together, the aircraft completed 356 flights, 1,286 hours of ground testing and 912 hours of flight testing. Much of the flight testing was based at Boeing Field in Seattle, Washington. The JAA process did not exist when the FAA certified the 757-200 in December 1982.
March 19, 1999	German carrier Condor Flugdienst commenced operations with the Boeing 757-300.
April 20, 1999	The first 757-200 equipped with upgraded avionics was delivered to Icelandair. The upgrade included a new flight management computer, a GPS that uses satellite signals to navigate during most phases of flight, a satellite communications system, the new enhanced ground proximity warning system, a predictive windshear system, and a new weather radar.
September 1999	British Airways announced that 34 of its then 53-aircraft 757 fleet would be sold to DHL for conversion into freighters.
October 5, 1999	Boeing and DHL launched a freighter conversion and fleet management programme. As part of this total solution, Boeing Airplane Services purchased 44 in-service 757 passenger aircraft, converted them to Special Freighter (SF) models, and provided the aircraft to DHL under a multi-year lease arrangement.
October 25, 1999	Delta Air Lines and Boeing celebrated Delta's 100th new 757-200.
May 2, 2000	American Airlines announced an order for 20 Boeing 757-200s, pushing the 757 programme beyond 1,000 to 1,009 aircraft.
July 11, 2000	The first Boeing 757-200 arrived at its Wichita, Kansas, facility for the DHL freighter conversion programme.
July 31, 2000	Modification of the first Boeing 757 passenger-to-freighter begins.
November 1, 2000	The side cargo door was installed on the first 757-200 to undergo passenger-to-freighter modification for DHL Worldwide Express at Boeing Airplane Services' Wichita facility.
February 1, 2001	In the first month of 2001, cumulative orders for the latest Boeing 757-300 more than doubled, with 33 confirmed orders for the single-aisle aircraft.
February 15, 2001	The first Boeing 757 Special Freighter (SF) made its maiden flight at Boeing Airplane Services' Wichita, Kansas, facility. Modification involved removal of the passenger furnishings, installation of a side cargo door, replacement of selected floor panels to strengthen the main deck floor, and installation of a cargo handling system.
March 2, 2001	Boeing celebrated the roll out of the first 757 Special Freighter (SF) for DHL Worldwide Express at Boeing Airplane Services' Wichita facility, where it was modified from a passenger jetliner to a freighter.
March 21, 2001	Boeing 757 in final assembly at Boeing's Renton, Washington facility. In the future, the fuselage of the aircraft would be assembled in Wichita, Kansas, and shipped by train to Renton for final assembly.
April 24, 2001	Boeing delivered the first Boeing 757-300 to operate in the United Kingdom to JMC Airlines, a Manchester, England-based charter carrier.
July 3, 2001	Northwest Airlines took delivery of its 50th new Boeing 757-200 on July 2, 2001.
December 20, 2001	Boeing delivered the first 757-300 to Continental Airlines, making the airline the first worldwide to operate the 757-300 in a dual-class configuration.
February 14, 2002	Boeing delivered the 1,000th 757 to American Airlines, the 148th in its fleet.
February 20, 2002	The first Boeing 757-300 aircraft powered by two Pratt & Whitney PW2040 engines made its maiden flight from Renton, Washington on the 20th anniversary of the first flight of the first 757-200.
July 15, 2002	Northwest Airlines took delivery of the first of 16 757-300s, marking another milestone in the largest fleet renewal programme in the carrier's 75-year history.
August 15, 2002	Boeing began assembling 757s on a moving assembly line in its Renton, Washington factory. The moving line method moved an aircraft 24 feet a day through the final assembly stage pulled by an automatic self-guided tug.
April 30, 2004	Boeing delivered the last 757-300 to Continental Airlines. Launched in 1996, the 757-300, at 178ft 7 in, is the longest single-aisle twinjet ever produced.
April 30, 2004	Boeing announced it was to finish production of 757 in late 2004 reflecting the market reality for the 757 as well as the growth in range and seating capacity of the Next-Generation 737 family.
October 28, 2004	Boeing rolled out the 1,050th 757, the last 757 ever to be built, from its Renton, Washington facility. The jet was delivered to Shanghai Airlines in 2005. Over the 23-year production run, 757s were delivered to 55 customers.
May 2005	The FAA certified winglets for the Boeing 757. They provided a 5% improvement in fuel efficiency, while boosting range by 200 nautical miles.
November 2014	Monarch retired the Boeing 757 with the type flying its final flights on November 2, 2014. Monarch took delivery of its first 757 in 1983, one of the first airlines in the world to operate the type.

The Renton production line with jets for Delta (3), British Airways (1) and Northwest (1).
BOEING

were re-examining their fleet portfolios. Northwest Orient Airlines placed an order, breaking a three-year 757 sales drought, although it was not until the end of the decade that orders per year edged closer to the 100 mark, as customers in other parts of the world began to realise the potential of the 757, amid increasing airline hub congestion and the introduction of airport noise regulations at US facilities.

Three's a Crowd?

During the 1970s, the US airline industry experienced a huge amount of change. With the advent of improved technology, manufacturers started to promote the idea of two-crew cockpits to airlines, much to the disapproval of pilots' unions. The Boeing 757 and 767 – which were developed concurrently – were designed to have identical cockpits, meaning pilots could fly both types on a common rating.

Both types were also intended to be operated by just two pilots and would be the second and third aircraft types in Boeing's line-up, after the 737, to have this capability.

Despite taking delivery of its first 737 in February 1968, United Airlines was forced to operate the type with three crew members until 1981.

As a result of this pushback, the 757 nearly kept its third crew member when launch customer Eastern Air Lines – under pressure from unions – agreed to retain the position.

"We had a policy on the books at the time, that any new or future jets irrespective of the number of engines, had to have a three-person crew   ➤

A Rolls-Royce RB211-535E4 is lifted into position for the engine hang. BOEING

with full duties and responsibilities with a panel for the flight engineer," explained George Jehn, a former Eastern Air Lines pilot and labour leader. "We bickered with Frank Borman [Eastern CEO] for a long time and finally he agreed to have a three-man crew on a 757".

The former pilot revealed that he and members of the Air Line Pilots Association (ALPA) flew to Seattle and toured a 757 simulator which included a fully installed flight engineer's panel.

"For some reason, when the ALPA board of directors – which included [officials] from all the airlines that the union represented – met that year [in the mid-1970s], two of them including Hawaiian Airlines and North Central Airlines wanted to have a two-pilot crew on the MD-80 [another two-crew designed jet]," George explained. "It was a year when the ALPA president, John O'Donnell was running for re-election, so he agreed to have a presidential commission decide the crew complement issue and of course, we knew where that was going. As we

predicted, the presidential panel came out in favour of a two-man crew."

As a result, when launch customer Eastern took delivery of the world's first Boeing 757 on December 22, 1982, it was handed over configured with just two positions on the flight deck.

From that point on, the decision to adopt a crew complement of two pilots led to the widespread adoption of this setup across all future airliners around the world.

The Seattle Rocket

Despite the sluggish start to sales, Boeing knew it was on to a winner based on feedback from early operators and passengers. For those handling the 757, the first impression was one of size, giving the illusion of being a widebody, sitting as it does much higher than other comparable aircraft on its tall undercarriage. This design feature was necessary to accommodate the generously proportioned engines, which also appear to be larger than needed. However, the thrust they provide gives the aircraft a power-to-weight ratio which at the time was only exceeded by Concorde, and pilots often refer to its rocket-like performance. A Boeing 757 can lift-off the runway in as little as 4,000ft, with a rotation speed of 140kts.

After 23 years, production of the 757 came to a halt in October 2004, with 1,050 aircraft produced.

The final delivery was to Shanghai Airlines which accepted the jet in 2005 after the aircraft spent a short spell in storage. Registered B-2876 (c/n 33967), it was the 13th 757-200 delivered to the Chinese carrier, which took delivery of its first example in August 1989. The aeroplane was transferred to Delta Air Lines in 2016 where it continues to fly as N823DX on a diverse range of transcontinental sorties.

While the 727 has largely disappeared from our skies, it seems the 757, with its new lease of life as a freighter will be around for many years. Even in its traditional passenger form, the 757 plays a major role for many big-name airlines. The pandemic flushed out many passenger examples from active fleets, but a notable number remain in service. ✈

Remaining
Peerless

The multi-purpose Boeing 757 remains peerless more than 40 years after its first flight. **Mark Broadbent** charts its history and considers operator options to replace the enduring all-rounder.

Whether flying bleary-eyed passengers on early morning trips across the Atlantic, shuttling freight between cargo hubs or ferrying holidaymakers across Europe, few types of airliner undertake such a variety of tasks as the Boeing 757. Add transporting VIPs, supporting humanitarian operations, or trialling new technologies to its CV and the effectiveness of the multi-tasker cannot be overstated.

Yet, this stalwart of the commercial aircraft scene does not rank highly on the list of the biggest-selling airliners. The total 1,049 production examples delivered to customers from 1983 to 2005 pales against other types.

Despite the arrival of new-generation midsize aircraft with better efficiency, the 757 is not easily replaceable. With useful life remaining in many, others finding new uses and the withdrawal of the type expected to be a relatively slow process, it appears set to remain a mainstay of the commercial aircraft industry.

Original 757-200

The initial variant was the 757-200, which entered service with Eastern Air Lines in January 1983 following certification. It is certified for a maximum capacity of 239 seats, »

Delta Air Lines Boeing 757-200 N712TW (c/n 27624) seen at Los Angeles International Airport is one of 113 currently in service.
AIRTEAMIMAGES/ENDA BURKE

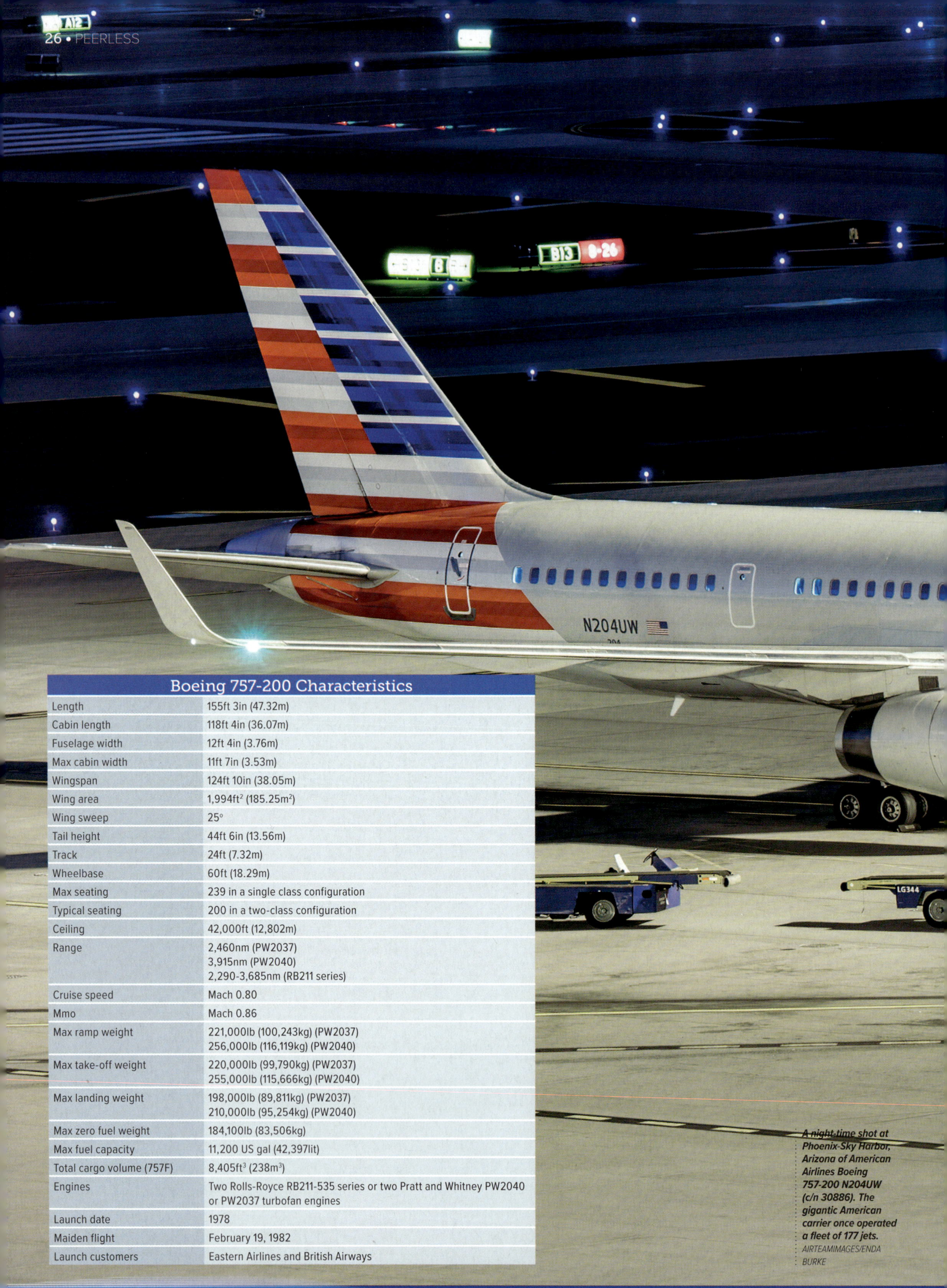

A night-time shot at Phoenix-Sky Harbor, Arizona of American Airlines Boeing 757-200 N204UW (c/n 30886). The gigantic American carrier once operated a fleet of 177 jets.
AIRTEAMIMAGES/ENDA BURKE

Boeing 757-200 Characteristics

Length	155ft 3in (47.32m)
Cabin length	118ft 4in (36.07m)
Fuselage width	12ft 4in (3.76m)
Max cabin width	11ft 7in (3.53m)
Wingspan	124ft 10in (38.05m)
Wing area	1,994ft^2 (185.25m^2)
Wing sweep	25°
Tail height	44ft 6in (13.56m)
Track	24ft (7.32m)
Wheelbase	60ft (18.29m)
Max seating	239 in a single class configuration
Typical seating	200 in a two-class configuration
Ceiling	42,000ft (12,802m)
Range	2,460nm (PW2037) 3,915nm (PW2040) 2,290-3,685nm (RB211 series)
Cruise speed	Mach 0.80
Mmo	Mach 0.86
Max ramp weight	221,000lb (100,243kg) (PW2037) 256,000lb (116,119kg) (PW2040)
Max take-off weight	220,000lb (99,790kg) (PW2037) 255,000lb (115,666kg) (PW2040)
Max landing weight	198,000lb (89,811kg) (PW2037) 210,000lb (95,254kg) (PW2040)
Max zero fuel weight	184,100lb (83,506kg)
Max fuel capacity	11,200 US gal (42,397lit)
Total cargo volume (757F)	8,405ft^3 (238m^3)
Engines	Two Rolls-Royce RB211-535 series or two Pratt and Whitney PW2040 or PW2037 turbofan engines
Launch date	1978
Maiden flight	February 19, 1982
Launch customers	Eastern Airlines and British Airways

PHOENIX
SKY HARBOR
INTERNATIONAL
AIRPORT
American
swissport

has a 255,00lb (116,000kg) maximum take-off weight (MTOW) and 3,850nm (7,130km) range with a full payload. Engines used include the Rolls-Royce RB211-535E4/E4B and the Pratt & Whitney PW2037 and PW2040.

Boeing built 913 757-200s. Many of these aircraft, especially those with the 'big three' mainline US carriers – Delta Air Lines, United Airlines and American Airlines – were later equipped with Aviation Partners Boeing (APB) Blended Winglets to improve their performance.

These devices were developed in the late 1990s, initially for the 737NG, to reduce the induced drag disrupting the efficient circulation of air around the wing. They were later approved for the 757 and the equipped aircraft were designated 757-200W or 757-200WL. As well as cutting fuel burn, the winglets extend range from the basic 3,915nm (7,250km) to 4,100nm (7,600km).

Stretched 757-300

The last new 757 variant was the stretched-fuselage 757-300, which entered service with Condor in 1999. The variant combines the 757-200's basic design with an extended fuselage: at 178ft 7in (54.5m) it is the longest single-aisle twinjet yet built.

Its extra length means it features a retractable tailskid on the aft fuselage to avoid tail strikes. The model carries up to 280 passengers as standard, with a maximum certified capacity of 295, a higher MTOW of 272,500lb

Icelandair now operates a fleet of 757-200s including TF-FIR (c/n 26242), though the fleet is due to be retired by 2026. AIRTEAMIMAGES/ EUROPIX

(124,000kg) and 3,395nm (6,290km) range.

The 757-300 was specifically designed to serve the charter airline market and launch operator Condor ordered it specifically to serve its high-density holiday routes. The variant is also used by Delta (which absorbed aircraft ordered by Northwest Airlines), and United Airlines.

Why is the 757 so Popular?

With more seats than single-aisles but fewer than the smallest twin-aisle widebodies, the 757 was designed principally to let airlines add capacity to high-frequency short- and medium-haul shuttle services in the US.

Initially, the 'big three' US carriers used their 757s predominantly on high-density trunk routes, and they continue to operate the type on some of their transcontinental services.

Charter operators elsewhere have used 757s to serve high-demand routes. Similarly, as a freighter the 757 provides capacity along 'the spokes' from the regional hubs of cargo carriers, thereby complementing the larger widebody types they use to fly intercontinental routes.

When the author spoke with UPS Airlines, the carrier had rostered 757s to fly from its European hub in Cologne to Stockholm, from its main Worldport hub in Louisville to Jacksonville, from Miami to Managua and from Shenzhen to Clark International in the Philippines.

The 757's range also means it can fly intercontinental services while European operators have long used the type to operate seasonal routes to Caribbean and US East Coast destinations.

The Right Size

The type's range has also enabled the 757 to fill a niche: operating so-called 'thin' transatlantic routes – the services from the US majors' large US East Coast hubs to secondary »

European destinations, where passenger volumes are insufficient to justify using a higher capacity widebody.

Network airlines must also manage seasonal shifts in passenger travel patterns and the 757's characteristics give carriers a useful tool in 'right-sizing'. Its size and range enable a route to continue if demand drops and makes larger-capacity aircraft too expensive.

The 757's utility in this respect is not limited to passenger carriers. A UPS Airlines spokesman explained to the author: "They're the only narrowbody freighters in our fleet, so we match them to the capacity needs on a particular route. It's very easy to swap tails and adjust capacity up or down on a particular day as necessary."

Icelandair is another example of the 757's right-sizing value. In recent years this carrier has expanded from Reykjavík as it seeks to establish its base as an alternative transfer hub between Europe and North America. Its 757-200s offer range to serve long-haul routes on both continents but do so without the risk of deploying too much capacity.

Flexibility

The 757's specific mix of midsize capacity, range, extended twin-engine operations clearance and short-field take-off and landing performance is also ideal for aircraft, crew, maintenance, and insurance (ACMI) charter specialists.

John Mahon, who flew the aircraft with now-defunct ACMI specialist Astraeus, told the author: "It's just so flexible. We did things with it that other aircraft couldn't do. Because the 757 has a four-bogie undercarriage, we were able to go into much smaller airports. We took the 757 into some interesting places."

For instance, an Astraeus 757 flew equipment and supplies into Haiti in the aftermath of the January 2010 earthquake. The 757 was the only civil aircraft allowed to land there after the quake, Mahon pointed out.

He also recalled: "I got a phone call saying, 'We need an airplane and crew to go down to South America and fly up to Miami via Aruba', a small island off the coast of South America in the Dutch Antilles."

Mahon said the 757 "was ideal for the task". The runway at the island's Queen Beatrix International Airport is 8,999ft (2,743m) long, but the 757-200 can take off in just 6,800ft (2,070m), enabling it to comfortably operate from Aruba yet also provide the range the tasking required. Delta and American have also operated 757s to the island from Miami.

A more unusual 757 charter was to provide aircraft for Iron Maiden tours (lead singer Bruce Dickinson was a qualified commercial pilot with the carrier). Two separate aircraft became the so called *Ed Force One*: firstly G-OJIB (c/n 24292, now a freighter with FedEx Express as N938FD) in 2008-2009, and then G-STRX (c/n 25621, now stored as EI-ETR) in 2011.

Fleet Changeovers

Operating the 757 presents a conundrum. The type has useful capabilities and gives carriers a lot of flexibility. It also has another, less

German carrier Condor has a fleet of 13 757-300s of which eight are currently operating flight services. This Condor Boeing 757-300 is seen at Palma de Mallorca.
AIRTEAMIMAGES/JONAS EVRARD

obvious benefit: because it has been in service for a long time its capital expenditure (capex) has been absorbed, so it has low ownership costs compared to newer aircraft.

However, older airliners are more expensive to fuel and maintain, and the 'Seven-Five' does not compare favourably with newer aircraft. Airbus' A321LR/A321XLR, the long-range versions of the A321neo, use 25% less fuel than the 757, the manufacturer claims.

These new midsize jets have bagged hundreds of orders. The French all business class carrier La Compagnie has already substituted A321LRs for their 757-200s.

The last of four 757s wet-leased by Aer Lingus from ASL Airlines, EI-CJX (c/n 26160) was withdrawn by the Irish carrier in May 2020. Three had already left its fleet: EI-LBR (c/n 28167) and EI-LBS (now N726WN, c/n 27623) in late 2019 and EI-LBT (c/n 28170) in January 2020.

The changeover from the 757 is happening even among the big US carriers. By Spring 2025, United had cut its fleet of 757-200s to 40 and »

Boeing 757-300 Characteristics	
Length	178ft 7in (54.43m)
Cabin length	141ft 7in (42.15m)
Fuselage width	12ft 4in (3.76m)
Max cabin width	11ft 7in (3.53m)
Wingspan	124ft 10in (38.05m)
Wing area	1,994ft² (185.25m²)
Wing sweep	25°
Tail height	44ft 6in (13.56m)
Track	24ft (7.32m)
Wheelbase	60ft (18.29m)
Max seating	295 in a single class configuration
Typical seating	243 in a two-class configuration
Ceiling	42,000ft
Range	2,460nm (PW2037) 3,915nm (PW2040) 2,290-3,685nm (RB211 series)
Cruise speed	Mach 0.80
Mmo	Mach 0.86
Max ramp weight	221,000lb (100,243kg) (PW2037) 256,000lb (116,119kg) (PW2040)
Max take-off weight	220,000lb (99,790kg) (PW2037) 255,000lb (115,666kg) (PW2040)
Max landing weight	198,000lb (89,811kg) (PW2037) 210,000lb (95,254kg) (PW2040)
Max zero fuel weight	184,100lb (83,506kg)
Max fuel capacity	11,200 US gal (42,397lit)
Total cargo volume	2,370ft³
Engines	Two Rolls-Royce RB211-535 series or two Pratt and Whitney PW2040 or PW2037 turbofan engines
Launch date	September 1996
Maiden flight	August 2, 1998
Launch customers	Condor

American had completely phased out the type. United's A321XLRs will arrive in January, 2026.

The decision of when 757s are replaced is down to each individual operator, who must work out the optimal time to phase out their specific aircraft by trading off the upcoming maintenance requirements and costs on their jets against the capital expenditure cost of new aircraft.

With most 757s now more than 20 years old, the market is seemingly moving inexorably towards a new generation, as the A321LR/XLR's popularity indicates. However, it is a mark of the 757's usefulness that some operators plan to phase it out slowly.

United will replace its fleet over several years and Delta, which with 107 jets flies the most examples of any single operator, appears to be in no hurry to retire its Boeing narrowbodies. Back in December 2019, Wayne Gilbert West, Delta's chief operating officer and senior executive vice president, told investors: "Keep in mind the delivery cycles of our 757s [were] staggered. We've retired some already and we've got retirement plans, but a large portion of those are out in the more distant horizon."

Cargo operators will also use 757s for many years to come. FedEx's phased replacement of the 727 with the 757 was only completed in 2013 and similarly UPS intends to fly its 757s for decades.

Upgrades

A long-term commitment to the 757 is reflected by continued investment in the aircraft. In 2013, APB introduced the Scimitar Blended Winglet (SBW) to the 757, which replaces the Blended Winglet's aluminium cap with a sharply swept-back tip and adds an aerodynamic trailing-edge wedge to the lower part of the winglet.

The SBW reduces fuel burn by an extra 1.1% and by 6% compared to a 757 without winglets, APB claims. Icelandair and United have retrofitted their 757s with the scimitar tips.

Meanwhile, Collins Aerospace (formerly Rockwell Collins) and Boeing offer a flight deck retrofit for the 757 which replaces six cathode ray tube displays with large-format (15.1in/383mm) LCD screens.

UPS Airlines is upgrading its 757s (and its 767s, with which the 757 has a common type rating) with the system. The carrier told the author: "The project is driven by the obsolescence of cathode ray tubes. Soon they just won't be available any longer, so we either had to stockpile CRTs or upgrade. We also expect the LCD displays to be more reliable."

Several airlines have also updated their 757 cabins. Most of American's

jets now have an all-business class cabin with lie-flat seats and Wi-Fi connectivity, both Delta and United have installed new slimline seats on their aircraft, and Icelandair added new seats, LED lighting and Global Eagle Entertainment satcom systems offering gate-to-gate Wi-Fi.

All these investments show that many operators believe the 757 will continue to serve them well for a long time to come, despite the emergence of new midsize aircraft.

As John Mahon put it: "Nothing compares to the 757 in terms of ability. The 757 does things other aeroplanes can't."

A Pilot's View

Captain Ken Hoke is a UPS Airlines 757 and 767 pilot with more than 4,000 hours flying both types. He told the author: "The 757 is great fun to fly. The plane is nimble and has a nice, solid feel on the controls. It has the perfect combination of old-school systems and modern automation. When the autopilot is turned off, it's easy to fly.

"The 757-200PF has a small cockpit compared to passenger variants; the floor plan is optimised for freight. The crew entry door is better described as a hatch, and it's a bit of a squeeze to get into the pilot seats. But once strapped in, it's pure Boeing 757.

"In the 1980s, the 757 earned the nickname 'Atari Ferrari' because of its then state-of-the-art glass cockpit and excellent performance. It's a forgiving aircraft with outstanding crosswind landing characteristics that make it a pleasure to fly.

"Initial pilot reaction to the large-format display system [LDS] flight deck upgrade was very positive. Although the classic cockpits are well liked, crew members who previously flew more modern equipment missed the benefits of advanced displays. Those of us raised on older steam gauges were excited about the new features available with LDS. As more aircraft are converted, maintaining currency is easier. For an old-timer like me, the first few flights in an LDS aircraft were a fun challenge. LDS provides more information to the pilots. And it's all good info. Speed tapes, trend vectors, improved traffic collision and avoidance system [TCAS] guidance, flight path vectors, and more, improve situational awareness. All this new data requires a different visual scan. It takes time and concentration to adapt.

"The Collins LDS is intuitive. After only a few flights, I preferred the LDS cockpit; and our flight crews will soon enjoy the benefits on every flight. I may be a fan of antiques, but I won't miss the classic Seven-Five instrument panel."

Condor 757-300 D-ABOL (c/n 29021) operating on a charter flight at Tenerife airport.
AIRTEAMIMAGES/MOISES MENDOZA

A day to REMEMBER

After 42 years of British passenger operations, Jet2 had the honour of operating the Boeing 757's final UK-scheduled passenger flights in January, 2025. *Airliner World* magazine's **Lee Cross** and **Thomas Haynes** were on board to experience the historic occasion.

Jet2's history with the Boeing 757 began in 2005, just two years after the airline's launch, when it acquired G-LSAA and G-LSAB. The following year, after seemingly being bitten by the bug, it acquired seven more 757s – G-LSAC through to AI.

Following the arrival of the tenth airframe, G-LSAJ, in May 2008, that October saw Jet2 launch direct flights to New York from its Leeds Bradford base using the 757. Initially operating four services during November and December, it was soon expanded across its other UK hubs. Alpha Kilo arrived in January 2010, followed by Alpha Lima and Alpha Mike in February and March 2011, respectively.

The latter pair left the fleet in October 2012 and were transferred to US carrier Allegiant Air. The 14th example, Alpha November, arrived in May 2012. The retirement of Alpha Golf in November 2019 signalled the slow and steady exit of the 757 from the fleet, as they were withdrawn from use by the leisure carrier. In May 2023, the airline acquired its 15th and final 757, G-LSAO, which would never fly for the airline and was instead cannibalised for parts.

When TUI Airways retired its final 757 on October 3, 2021, it left Jet2 as the only remaining British passenger operator of the type. Just two months earlier, the latter had placed an order with Airbus for 15 A321neo aircraft, and the writing was on the wall for the Seattle Rocket.

Final call for landmark flights

Amber weather warnings for snow and ice, and technical issues with the aircraft the previous day, meant that everything seemed to be against us for the penultimate 757 flight, LS811, from Manchester to Geneva on the morning of January 5, 2025 (Lee Cross writes). After a slow and somewhat treacherous drive, I sailed through security and soon found myself sitting in Terminal 2 departures with a large coffee, watching the snow get deeper across the airfield. Unsurprisingly, the airport announced that it had temporarily closed.

Jet2 flight LS811 taxiing past Terminal 2 at Geneva ahead of the last-ever flight back to Manchester.
KEY-THOMAS HAYNES

The last three 757s to be retired by Jet2 lined up for a photoshoot on runway 23L at Manchester. JET2

RIGHT •
Lee was seated in 38A, which is positioned behind the mid-cabin toilets. *KEY-LEE CROSS*

BELOW RIGHT •
A snow-covered Alpha India ahead of her flight to Geneva. *KEY-LEE CROSS*

Despite the setback, boarding began promptly from gate B9 at 0555hrs. At the gate, it became clear what a moment in aviation history this was, as the mix of aviation enthusiasts and regular passengers came together. The latter, of course, had no idea what an occasion this was but as the two groups mingled and chatted, this quickly changed as both sides shared their memories of the iconic jet.

Our 757-21B, G-LSAI was parked on a remote stand. After boarding the bus, it was only as we crawled across the apron that the full extent of the snow became apparent. Then, out of the gloom, there she was. The oldest commercial passenger Boeing 757 still in service, looking resplendent

in Jet2's silver and red livery, albeit covered in a blanket of snow. I was the first off the bus into the biting wind and snow that was now turning to sleet. Some people raced straight to the stairs, which were positioned, unusually for a 757, at door 1L. In the company of countless others, I tried to capture as many images as possible of the 37-year-old jet. Before long though the cold had got to us all, and we edged our way up the stairs to the warm and inviting glow of the cabin. We were greeted by the exceptional cabin crew. All five senior cabin crew members had been with the company for many years and were specially selected by management for this historic occasion.

I made my way down to seat 38A, located in the small cabin at the rear »

behind the mid-cabin toilets. Despite the aircraft's age, the interior was immaculate and a credit to the airline's engineering teams. The only thing that gave away Alpha India's history was the Chinese writing on the passenger service units from its CAAC/China Southern Airlines days.

With everyone onboard, the doors were closed and captain David Rix, who was joined in the flight deck by fellow captain Charlie Collier, made his welcome onboard PA. He broke the news that the airport was not expected to reopen until 0900hrs. There were the usual groans from the non-enthusiast passengers, but for many, it meant we could spend some extra time with this aviation icon. Sadly, the announcement did not mention that this was the final departure from the UK of a British-registered passenger 757. However, captain Collier (who was flying this sector) hinted at the occasion when he offered to open the flight deck to passengers while on the ground. Those of us who wanted to visit the business end were asked to press our call bells, and immediately, a wave of 'dings' went off, with the cabin ceiling alight at almost every row.

Outside, the ground crews were busy clearing the snow from the airfield, and just after 0900hrs, the de-icing cherry picker arrived at the aircraft. Captain Collier informed the cabin that flight deck visits would now be suspended, much to the disappointment of those who had not yet had the privilege, including yours truly. Thankfully, we were then informed that we would be able to visit upon our arrival in Geneva.

De-icing complete, and after a slightly worrying moment when the steps returned to the aircraft – apparently to check a warning that the cabin door wasn't closed properly – we began our pushback a little after 0930hrs. The cabin crew carried out the obligatory

safety demo "for this Boeing 757 Luxury Liner", and soon we were taxiing out to Manchester's now cleared runway 05L. An easyJet Airbus A320 beat us to be the first aircraft to leave that morning, and while we believed that we would be second, a short stop on the taxiway saw one of the Jet2's brand new A320neos, G-SUNG (c/n 11799), ironically the type that is replacing the 757, move ahead of us.

Then it was our turn. At 1003hrs, Alpha India lined up on the runway for the final time, (with passengers onboard at least). The Rolls-Royce RB211 engines were spooled up to full power while the brakes were held; a standard procedure owing to the runway surface conditions. After a few moments, the brakes were released and we were pinned into our seats as the aircraft raced down the runway, becoming airborne just past the Runway Visitor Park. Around the cabin, phones and cameras were pressed to the windows to capture the historic occasion as we soared into the gloomy skies, glimpsing the snow-covered Peak District before disappearing into the cloud base.

The flight itself was 'business as usual' for the cabin crew as they carried out the in-flight service. Around 20 minutes before our descent into Geneva, captain Collier made the

Jet2 Boeing 757 Fleet				
Reg	Type	c/n	Delivery Date	Notes
G-LSAA	Boeing 757-236	24122	04/10/2005	
G-LSAB	Boeing 757-27B	24136	30/07/2005	
G-LSAC	Boeing 757-23A	25488	14/03/2006	
G-LSAD	Boeing 757-236	24397	16/06/2006	
G-LSAE	Boeing 757-27B	24135	25/09/2006	
G-LSAF	Boeing 757-225	22689	30/10/2006	
G-LSAG	Boeing 757-21B	24014	23/11/2006	
G-LSAH	Boeing 757-21B	24015	05/02/2007	
G-LSAI	Boeing 757-21B	24016	23/11/2006	
G-LSAJ	Boeing 757-236	24793	06/05/2008	
G-LSAL	Boeing 757-204	26967	11/02/2011	Leased from Allegiant Air until October 2012
G-LSAM	Boeing 757-204	26966	12/04/2011	Leased from Allegiant Air until October 2012
G-LSAN	Boeing 757-2K2	26635	06/05/2012	
G-LSAK	Boeing 757-23N	27973	28/01/2010	
G-LSAO	Boeing 757-256	29309	16/05/2023	Acquired for parts
EC-ISY	Boeing 757-256	26241	20/05/2015	Leased from Privilege Style for 2015 summer season. Jet2 titles added to forward fuselage
G-POWH	Boeing 757-256	29308	19/03/2016	Leased from Titan Airways for 2016 and 2018 summer season. Jet2 titles added to forward fuselage

standard PA, detailing the flight so far, our cruising altitude (35,000ft), outside air temperature, and our arrival time. It was only then that the crew officially mentioned the important detail: that this was the penultimate passenger flight of a British-registered Boeing 757.

Soon, we began our final approach to Geneva. The weather outside was decidedly better than the weather we had left in the UK, and as we lined up with runway 22, we saw some incredible views of the Alps and, eventually, Lake Geneva.

One hour and 36 minutes after our take off from Manchester, Alpha India's wheels kissed the runway at Geneva. Sadly, there was no fanfare or round of applause for this momentous occasion. Instead, the cabin crew made the usual after-landing PA as we made our way to a remote stand in front of Terminal 2.

As passengers disembarked, many continued to take photos while those, like me, who had not managed to visit the flight deck earlier, awaited our turn.

ABOVE •
At 37 years old, G-LSAI was the oldest passenger Boeing 757 in the world.
KEY-THOMAS HAYNES

TOP •
During the boarding for LS812, passengers on the first bus were afforded a considerable amount of time to take in the moment.
KEY-THOMAS HAYNES

RIGHT •
The descent into Geneva provided a great view of the Alps
KEY-LEE CROSS

BELOW •
A view out the port side of the aircraft showcasing the smart red coloured engine nacelles with Jet2's signature silver inlet cowling
KEY-THOMAS HAYNES

When it was finally my turn to go up front and take the captain's seat for some photos, captain Collier was in the jumpseat, having adopted a new role as designated photographer for the enthusiastic visitors. After taking a few snaps, Collier told me that he had worked on the 757 for 19 years and that flying "a real pilot's aeroplane" had been a pleasure. He added that although he

was sad to see the type leave, he was now looking forward to "going back to school" to get trained on the new A321neo fleet.

With photos taken and only too aware of the crew's tight turnaround time, plus the plane load of very excited ticket holders, including *Airliner World* editor Thomas Haynes, itching to get onboard to take her back to ⟫

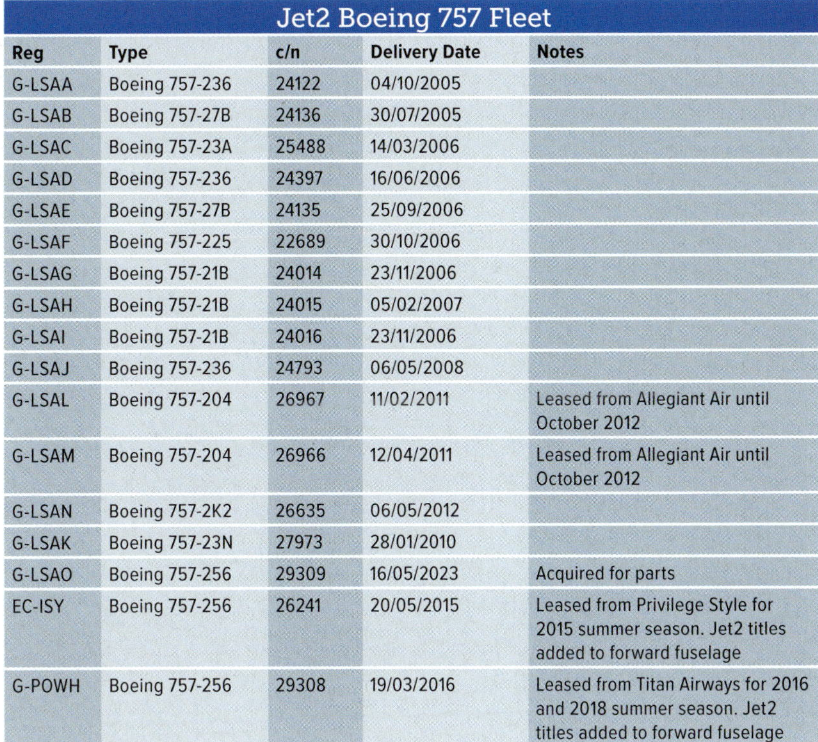

Manchester one final time, I made my way off the aircraft, grabbing a few more pictures as I went.

As a child of the eighties, the 757 was a constant in my life, whether it was taking my parents and I off on holiday or spotting the various liveries of its operators over the years. Hearing the roar of the RB211s as we raced off down the runway a couple of hours earlier is a moment I will always cherish.

Time to say goodbye

After 42 years, the end of passenger operations with British 757s was now in sight (Thomas Haynes writes). Those due on flight LS812 waited patiently for the aircraft to arrive at Geneva's gate D86. The sun had been threatening to show its face all morning, and as Alpha India lined up on final approach for runway 22, it finally brightened up outside, almost as though the weather understood the significance of the aircraft's arrival. Happily, as the 757 was due to park on a remote stand down at the airport's southern end, it meant it had to taxi straight past the gate, prompting the enthusiasts' cameras into a blitz of clicking like paparazzi snapping a film star.

Boarding began shortly thereafter and after enquiring with the Swissport ground staff, I was thankfully given back my pre-booked window seat – this was not a flight I wanted to find myself relegated to the middle seat for. A remote stand would normally be an inconvenience in my eyes, but for today's flight, it was the cherry on top. We arrived at the aircraft and our bus – which had somehow been exclusively filled with the enthusiast cohort – emptied in record time as we spilled out onto the apron with cameras at the ready. Unsurprisingly, no one seemed to get on the aircraft for several minutes as we all set about capturing the aircraft from every possible angle. Passengers eventually boarded the jet, only to drop their bags and get off again. After exhausting every photo opportunity and prompted by the arrival of the second bus, we started to take our assigned seats.

It was only as I settled into seat 28F – positioned just behind Alpha India's winglet-less starboard wing – that it

started to sink in that this was actually the last flight. Pushback commenced at 1430hrs local time, some three-and-a-half hours late owing to Manchester's weather; not that it mattered to most of the passengers – we were all just glad to be on board. Sadly, this take-off was derated, as per normal procedure, and with the RB211s roaring, we thundered down runway 22, lifting off into the Swiss skies. A right-hand turn after take-off once we passed around 7,000ft saw the passengers on the starboard side get a glimpse of the airport before we were enveloped by the cloud base.

The short sector length meant that the in-flight service was a bit of a rush for the crew, but they did their best to get through the whole cabin. I looked out the window for most of the flight, taking in the view of the wing that one last time; absorbing the experience as much as was humanly possible. Before long, captain Rix (who was flying this sector) came over the PA to provide an update on our progress. We were now over northern France, about to coast out into the English Channel near

The flight deck of G-LSAI has been upgraded over the years with more modern equipment to ensure continued compatibility with regulations. KEY-THOMAS HAYNES

Boulogne-sur-Mer, still at our cruising level of 38,000ft. We now only had 15 minutes left up at altitude, before a descent into Manchester would be initiated. Owing to our later departure, we were now chasing the sun as it began to set.

The seatbelt signs came on and while the crew set about preparing for arrival, I was mentally processing the fact that the flight – along with the passenger-carrying career of British 757s – was nearing its conclusion. By now, we were firmly 'in the soup' so there was nothing but grey to be seen out of the window. The light was beginning to fade as we emerged from beneath the cloud to be met by a very murky Manchester.

Touchdown! The ground spoilers rose up and reverse thrust began to roar as we rolled out on runway 05R. On our right-hand side at the perimeter fence, I could see gaggles of people braving the weather for the opportunity to witness history being made. Just like that, after 42 years of British 757 passenger operations, the last passenger flight had now been completed. A round of applause broke out through the

Touchdown! G-LSAI arrives into a wet Manchester. JET2

ABOVE •
Flight LS812 is marshalled onto stand. *JET2*

RIGHT •
Blasting out of Geneva. *KEY-THOMAS HAYNES*

cabin, with even the non-enthusiasts becoming drawn in to the festivities.

As we pulled onto stand, someone towards the front of the cabin called out "hip hip hooray", which got something of a lukewarm response. "Shall we do that again?" quipped another enthusiast, before a second much more forceful attempt garnered slightly more support. Outside, the rain poured down – fitting weather for such a sad occasion. The RB211s were shut down and the whine of the iconic turbofan lingered until it faded into the burble of the cabin. Passengers were invited to take the safety cards as a "memento" of the special occasion.

The aircraft emptied quickly as the non-enthusiast travellers dashed across the tarmac to the waiting buses. Once they'd gone, those who remained engaged in what I can only describe as a standoff. With the bus driver itching to depart, no one wanted to get off the aircraft because in doing so, we would seal the jet's fate. The long queue to visit the flight deck certainly didn't help matters, but people waited patiently for their turn to look at the business end. The crew were fantastically patient, and I couldn't help feeling guilty because

The crew for the final flight with captains Charlie Collier (left) and David Rix in the middle. *JET2*

their day – which had started in the very early hours of the morning – had been extended because of the delays at Manchester and was now being further stretched by our enthusiasm for the aircraft.

Amid a scramble by many to get the crew to sign safety cards and model aircraft, I managed to grab a few moments with captain Rix: "It's a sad occasion," he admitted. "Happy because I had the chance to fly this aeroplane which has been fantastic, but to see it go is quite emotional."

Rix has been with Jet2 since 2006 and had flown the 757 the whole time. "I've done everything I need to do on the 757," he added. "I was a line trainer, type rating examiner and I also managed the fleet – so I've done everything."

"It's been so nice to see everybody," enthused Rix. "There are so many

enthusiastic people that have come to see us. We're pilots; we get to fly it every day as a job, but for everybody else to see this aeroplane, and to enjoy it, is really nice."

By now, the bus driver's patience had worn thin, so our time on board had run out. After a quick dash into the flight deck to get one last picture, I made my way to door 2L. Stepping out into the rain, I glanced back as I descended the steps – taking it in that one last time.

It is no secret that the 757 is my favourite aircraft. While it's sad that the type's passenger-carrying duties for UK airlines have come to an end, I am heartened by the fact that its flying career more generally is far from over and it'll be many, many years before we see it disappear completely.

A growing number of Boeing 757 freighters serve the world's cargo carriers. **Jon Lake** charts the evolutionary course of this flexible freighter.

CARGO KING

DHL Air Boeing 757-200SF G-BMRJ (c/n 24268) at East Midlands Airport.
AIRTEAMIMAGES/ENDA BURKE

he Boeing 757 was designed as a replacement for the older Model 727, and it was perhaps inevitable that Boeing's new narrow-body would follow its trijet predecessor into the cargo market. Although wide-bodied aircraft were rapidly being pressed into use in the freighter role, especially on intercontinental routes, and though these were enjoying great popularity thanks to their capacious cabins, there was still a place for a smaller freighter to provide capacity along 'the spokes' that emanated from the cargo carriers' regional hubs. And the 757 promised to do so while offering much better fuel economy than the 727, and the ability to use shorter or hot and high runways.

757-200PF

Thus, just four years and nine months after Eastern Air Lines had put the passenger-carrying 757-200 into commercial service on January 1, 1983 the Boeing 757-200PF package freighter variant entered service with UPS in September 1987 and the 757-200M combi model followed suit with Nepal Airlines in September 1988.

The 757-200PF variant has a maximum take-off weight of 255,000lb (115,666kg) and a maximum range of 3,150nm (5,830km). In practise, this means that the 757-200PF can carry a maximum 86,900lb (39,417kg) load on the 6,600ft3 (187m3) main deck, swallowing up to 15 standard-sized (15 x 25in/381 x 635mm) containers. Loading and unloading is undertaken using an upward-opening freight door in the forward part of the fuselage on the port side just ahead of the wing. The main deck is augmented by two lower deck holds (one forward of the wings, one aft) providing a further 1,830ft3 (51.8m3) of space for bulk cargo.

The aircraft was built with most of the doors and windows of the passenger version omitted. The floor plan of the 757-200PF is optimised for freight, and the aircraft has a smaller cockpit compared to passenger variants. To access this a smaller crew entry door for the pilots was added near the cockpit windows, In place of the normal forward boarding door.

The new crew entry door is 'better described as a hatch', according to one pilot, who said that "it's a bit of a squeeze to get into the pilot seats. But once strapped in, it's pure Boeing 757!"

Only 80 aircraft were built as freighters on the Renton production line, but many more have been converted to freighter or combi standards by a number of companies, including Boeing itself.

Some 75 of the Boeing-built 757 freighters were delivered to United Parcel Service (UPS - with whom they remain in service), the first being Boeing 757-24APF N401UP (line number 139). All were powered by Pratt & Whitney PW2040 engines. The aircraft was delivered to UPS on October 6, 1987, and was pressed into service to deliver packages at night, loaded onto pallets or LD3 containers.

The Boeing 757-200PF has a total payload of 40 tonnes for medium-haul flights and can carry bulk goods with a volume of approximately 50m3. The aircraft is equipped with an auxiliary power unit for long-haul flights.

The next operator of the 757-200PF was Challenge Air Cargo, which

Boeing 757-200SF N967FD (c/n 26269) is one of 92 currently in service with FedEx Express. The jet seen at San Jose Airport in Costa Rica.
AIRTEAMIMAGES/JOSE SALAZAR

took delivery of three Rolls Royce RB211-535E4 powered aircraft from July 26, 1989, using the designation Boeing 757-23APF. The aircraft were leased from Ansett Worldwide – whose fourth 757-23APF initially went to Zambian Airlines. The next 757-200PF operator was Ethiopian Airlines, who would operate two dedicated freighter examples of the 757, powered by Pratt and Whitney PW2040 engines, alongside a dozen passenger versions. The first of these was a new-build 757-260PF, ET-AJS (line number 300), which joined Ethiopian on August 24, 1990. This made Ethiopian the first passenger-carrying airline to order and receive the freighter version of the 757. The aircraft served until June 2018, and remains in use with Asia Pacific Airlines.

The second Ethiopian 757 freighter was originally delivered as a passenger-configured aircraft in February 1991, serving the airline for 15 years before conversion to freighter configuration in 2006. It then flew cargo for Ethiopian for more than a decade, finally being withdrawn in October 2017.

The three aircraft delivered to Challenge Air Cargo served until late 1999/early 2000, and all found new operators in the shape of Icelandair, SNAS Aviation and European Air Transport.

The second Challenge aircraft went on to fly with Cameroon Airlines, Ansett, Icelandair, Arrow Air and others, finally ending up with Spain's Swiftair. The third aircraft has served mainly with different DHL partner carriers and remains in use with DHL Air Austria.

Two Boeing 757-29JAPF aircraft for Egypt's Shorouk Air were, in the end, not taken up.

The 757-24APF is now in its 35th year of operation with UPS, but the aircraft are being upgraded for continued service, receiving a Collins Aerospace (formerly Rockwell Collins) and Boeing-designed flight deck upgrade. This will see six obsolescent cathode ray tube (CRT) displays being replaced by more reliable large-format (15.1in) LCD screens. Much the same upgrade is being applied to the carrier's Boeing 767s (which share a common type rating with the 757).

Captain Ken Hoke, a UPS Airlines Boeing 757 and 767 pilot, told AIR International that: "The Collins LDS is intuitive. After only a few flights, I prefer the LDS cockpit; and our flight crews will soon enjoy the benefits on every flight. I may be a fan of antiques, but I won't miss the classic Seven-Five instrument panel. "Initial pilot reaction to the large-format display system [LDS] flight deck upgrade was very »

positive. Although the classic cockpits are well liked, crew members who previously flew more modern equipment missed the benefits of advanced displays. Those of us raised on older 'steam gauges' were excited about the new features available with LDS," Hoke said. "As more aircraft are converted, maintaining currency is easier. "For an old-timer like me, the first few flights in an LDS aircraft were a fun challenge. LDS provides more information to the pilots. And it's all good info. Speed tapes, trend vectors, improved traffic collision and avoidance system [TCAS] guidance, flight path vectors, and more, improve situational awareness. All this new data requires a different visual scan. It takes time and concentration to adapt."

Conversions

The 80 new build 757-200PFs and a single Combi 757-200M were augmented by about 317 aircraft (so far) converted to freighter or Combi standards from 757-200 airliners. These passenger to freighter (P2F) conversions have been undertaken by a range of engineering companies – including Boeing itself.

There were three main Supplementary Type Certificates (STCs) covering 757 freighter conversions, resulting in slightly different aircraft configurations, though all start by adding a cargo door on the port forward fuselage (identical to that fitted to the new-build 757-200PF), and by removing all passenger amenities. Most cabin doors are sealed shut, and cabin windows are blanked off.

The original Boeing STC covered the original 757-200SF conversion – beginning with the 29 former British Airways 757-236s converted to 757SF standards at Wichita and Tel Aviv/Ben Gurion for DHL. Five of these remain in service.

The Boeing STC was sold to IAI in conjunction with Singapore Technologies (ST Aero)/Mobile Aerospace (MAE) and was subsequently refined and improved.

The second STC was developed by Alcoa/SIE and resulted in the 14Plus B757-200ASF configuration. This STC was subsequently acquired by Pemco World Air Services in Tampa, Florida. Confusingly, both Boeing/IAE/ST Aero/Mobile Aerospace and Alcoa/Pemco conversions tend to be designated as 757-200SFs (Special Freighters).

The final 757 freighter STC was held by Precision Conversions (later Precision Aircraft Solutions), with the 757-200PCF – initially distinguished by being the first conversion able to carry 15 pallets, rather than 14 or 14.5.

The difference is primarily a product of door configuration – those conversions that retain the normal L1 entrance door had 14 positions for 125 x 88 pallets or ULD (unit load device) containers – sometimes with an additional 'half-size' 88x88 pallet in Position A. Optionally, the 757SF could accommodate 12 125 x 96in pallets by moving quick-release locks from the 88in to the 96in position.

Those conversions that removed the L1 door, and replaced it with a smaller, inward opening crew entry hatch, (like that of the production 727-200PF) recouped useful weight savings, reduced maintenance requirements and gained a full (15th) pallet position in Position A, more than justifying the expense of removing the entry door! The 757 freighter frequently ran out of space well before they reached their payload weight limit, so an extra pallet position was especially useful. The only downside, according to one pilot, was that the toilet was now on the flight deck.

Partners

Boeing undertook freighter conversions in association with a number of partners, including ST Aero and IAI (for aircraft destined for DHL), and ST Aero alone (for aircraft destined for FedEx).

Singapore Technologies Engineering, or ST Aero, then claimed to be the "world's largest commercial airframe MRO provider," and was involved in passenger-to-freighter conversions for many years, principally as a provider of touch labour for Boeing rather than as a developer of its own conversion programmes. This began to change in 2007 when ST Aero signed a deal with FedEx for 87 (later 119) Boeing 757-200SF freighters, these featuring a 14-pallet configuration. ST (through its subsidiary VT Mobile Aerospace Engineering) delivered the last of these aircraft in mid-2015. VT MAE was established in September 1990 by ST Engineering and is located at Brookley Aeroplex in Mobile, Alabama, and at the Pensacola International Airport in Pensacola, Florida

ST Aero's contract for 119 conversions for FedEx means that the company has converted more 757-200s to freighter configuration than any of its competitors. But almost all of those were aircraft configured to carry 14 pallets, and so, as the end of the contract approached ST Aerospace began work on certification of its own 15-pallet conversion. In early 2016, ST Aero received certification for a 15-pallet 757-200 P-to-F conversion, and delivered five conversions to launch customer SF Airlines from 2018.

Another 757 freighter STC was granted to Alcoa-SIE Cargo Conversions' (ASCC), which produced its first '14Plus' 757-200SF conversion for Babcock & Brown

Aircraft Management in 2005. The aircraft was delivered from the conversion facility - Commercial Jet at Miami International Airport in Miami, Florida, a sister company of Aeronautical Engineers (AEI) - in January 2007. The 14Plus configuration was claimed to offer 97% of the pallet volume of the 15-pallet configuration (and the same payload weight) at 80% of the cost.

ASCC's 14Plus offered a simpler design that retained more of the Boeing 757-200's original structure and systems, thereby significantly reducing conversion time and cost while retaining an area for Supernumeraries, three coach class seats, together with a full galley and lavatory.

In 2010, the 757 cargo conversion operations and assets of Alcoa-SIE Conversions (ASCC) were acquired by Pemco World Air Services, and thereafter were marketed as a Pemco product. ASCC president Robert Murphy noted that the 757 freighter would "round out the product portfolio in the Pemco family of narrowbody cargo aircraft options," and said that he was "pleased to see the highly efficient conversion design that ASCC has pioneered incorporated into the product line of one of the world's most experienced cargo conversion companies."

757-200PCF

In 2001, Oregon-based Erickson Air-Crane created Precision Conversions as a new, standalone business to undertake the engineering, prototyping, and certification of a new 15-pallet 757-200 passenger-to-freighter conversion programme – the Boeing 757-200PCF.

The new version featured a Class E cargo compartment with a reinforced floor structure, a seven-track ANCRA cargo handling system, and a rigid 9G barrier. The aircraft was able to carry 15 88 x 125in or 88 x 108in pallets or 13 larger 96 x 125in pallets or containers on the main deck. The flight deck had seating for up to six and a new crew lavatory installation.

Precision claims that the B757-200PCF is the market leader with the lowest operating empty weight (115,500–116,000lb) and the highest available payload (up to 84,000lb) of any 757-freighter conversion. This makes it 1,500–1,800lb lighter than the competition, and Precision offers additional significant optional weight upgrades.

The Precision B757-200PCF has been certified by the FAA, and EASA, and in Brazil, Canada, China, and Russia, with over 153 delivered and 134 in active service around the world.

The 757-freighter proved popular as a replacement for the trijet Boeing 727 and the four-engine DC-8 aircraft, offering higher capacity and greatly improved fuel efficiency. The 757 has been particularly relevant to the European market because of its capacity and range, but has also been heavily used in the United States and China.

In late 2021, *Aviation Business News* reported that the Boeing 757-200 continued to be the "pre-eminent candidate for conversion" in the large narrow body segment, though *Air Cargo News* noted the emergence of a new rival. It pointed out that although ten aircraft had been converted in 2020, with eight more in 2021, and an additional 30 due to be converted in the future, "conversions of the Airbus A321-200 are now growing with three so far in 2021, three in 2020, and with a further 19 set to be converted in the future." This could suggest that the 757 will soon lose its crown as King of the narrow body freighters.

Passengers, Cargo, or Both

Jon Lake reviews the Boeing 757 Combi aircraft, a variant configured to transport either passengers, freight, or a combination of both.

At one time, it was possible to certify airliners that could carry a variable mix of passengers and cargo on their main deck – with a moveable bulkhead between the two. But these Combi airliners no longer meet modern certification standards. Instead, a fixed bulkhead is now deemed necessary between the cargo area and the passenger area. In the event of a fire, this configuration is a means to contain fire away from the passengers. Halon or CO2 can be used to extinguish the fire without affecting them. This means a modern Combi can only have a fixed capacity passenger area on the main deck.

The modern alternative to a traditional Combi is a quick-change freighter that can be speedily reconfigured for all-cargo or all-passenger operations, removing the seats to turn an aircraft into a freighter, or refitting them to produce an airliner. Such aircraft are not well optimised for passenger operations, as the cargo door will often leak cold air and noise into the cabin, and overhead baggage compartments can't usually be installed around the cargo door. At the same time, the overhead compartments, lavatories, and galleys take up useful space that would otherwise be available for cargo.

Programme Effect

The demise of the Combi as a concept had a significant effect on the 757 programme. Boeing built only a single example of its new-build, new production Combi (generically known as the 757-200M) for Nepal Airlines as the sole Boeing 757-2F8M. This aircraft made its maiden flight on July 15, 1988 and was delivered to Nepal that September.

This aircraft was fitted with the 757-200PF's forward port-side cargo door as well as provision for a full passenger interior and had the normal window arrangement. The 757-200M was convertible between the freighter and passenger roles, and could operate in a mixed configuration, able to carry between two and four cargo pallets on its main deck, along with up to 148 passengers in the remaining cabin space. It served from Tribhuvan International Airport in Kathmandu until withdrawn from use on September 30, 2018 when it passed to CSDS Aircraft Sales and Leasing.

The sole production Boeing 757-200M was joined by just six civil Combi conversions, all with a fixed bulkhead between the freight and passenger compartments. With a set space for freight, that would never be used for passengers, these aircraft had their forward passenger windows removed and faired over, leaving just 13 windows aft, on each side.

The first 757s converted to anything approaching a Combi configuration were the pair delivered to the Royal New Zealand Air Force in April and June 2003 and discussed at length in the 'Four Winds' chapter. From 2007 these underwent modifications at the hands of Mobile Aerospace Engineering, who installed an upper deck cargo door and a strengthened floor in order to allow the carriage of large and heavy cargo, with an 11-pallet cargo capability. The aircraft also gained internal air stairs, upgraded engines and flight deck enhancements. As military transport aircraft, they did not require a fixed bulkhead between the freight and passenger compartments. Mobile Aerospace did produce one civil Combi, converting a former Air Finland aircraft for Guggenheim Aviation Partners, who subsequently leased the aircraft to TNT Airways from March 2011, and then, from May 2016, to SL Airlines Belgium. The aircraft was withdrawn from use at the end of 2018, and was then converted to full freighter configuration, losing its remaining cabin windows.

National Airlines

At much the same time that Mobile Aerospace was producing its civil Combi, Pemco World Air Services began converting four Boeing 757-200s to Combi configuration for National Airlines. The new 757-200C blended the company's 757 freighter conversion with a successful Pemco 737-400 Combi conversion for Alaska Airlines that Pemco had designed, built, and certified in 2006.

The Pemco World Air Services 757 Combi conversion included the installation of a large cargo door and freight handling system, a Class C cargo compartment with ten pallet positions and automatic fire detection and suppression. Further aft, Pemco installed an in-flight entertainment system in the 42-seat passenger compartment, two full galleys, and the aircraft gained a modern flight deck with state-of-the-art glass instrumentation.

The 757C launch project was originally expected to involve a total of five National Airlines aircraft, but in the event, only four were converted (becoming a Boeing 757-2Z0(C), a 757-2G5(C), and two 757-2Y0(C)s), achieving FAA certification in the first quarter of 2011.

Unique Bird

Wilmington-based Air Transport International has the two converted 757-2Y0(C) Combis, with another 757-2G5(C) . The fourth 757-2Z0(C) Combi conversion went to International Air Response. Rounding out the ATI fleet is a unique Combi – the sole Boeing 757-2Q8(PCC)(WL) which features the forward cockpit entry door of the PCF variant.

This former Aeromexico and SunExpress airliner became the only Precision Aircraft Solutions 757-200PCC Combi, differing from other Combi conversions in having the small crew entry hatch immediately behind the cockpit windows, and no standard forward entry door, like production 757-200APF freighters, and the converted 757-200PCF. The aircraft offers ten full cargo positions and seating for 54 passengers and is the only certified 757-200 Combi variant to include winglets.

Flight deck

BOEING 757

The first of five sections detailing the Boeing 757's major systems using excerpts from the 2010 issue of The Boeing Company's operating manual.

The Boeing 757's flight deck is equipped with an assortment of displays, the flight management and navigation systems, and the automatic flight control.

The electronic flight instrument system (EFIS) consists of three (left, centre, right) symbol generators (SGs), two control panels (CPs), two attitude director indicators (ADIs), two horizontal situation indicators (HSIs), and ambient light sensing units.

The EFIS uses information provided by a variety of aircraft systems to generate the appropriate visual presentations on the ADI and HSI. Data relating primarily to navigation is provided by aircraft systems such as the navigation radios, flight management computer (FMC), and the inertial reference systems. Data relating primarily to automatic flight is provided by the flight control computers (FCCs), the auto-throttle (AT), and the FMC.

Data which is used to display current aircraft state information is provided by two air data computers (ADCs) and three inertial reference systems (IRSs).

Display intensity is automatically adjusted for each display unit based on ambient light sensors.

Pilots control of the displays is achieved by positioning the various controls on the respective EFIS control panels to the desired settings. The controls panels are also used to control display options, modes, and ranges and brightness.

Three symbol generators receive inputs from various aircraft systems, then generate the proper visual displays for the related ADI and HSI. Each pilot's ADI and HSI displays are provided from the switch-selected SG. The left and right side SGs provide the captain's and the first officer's display respectively. The centre SG can be used by either pilot as an alternate source.

An attitude director indicator (ADI) presents conventional displays for attitude (pitch and roll throughout 360° of rotation in each axis), flight director commands, localiser deviation and glide slope deviation. In addition, the ADI displays information relating to auto-flight system mode annunciations, airspeed, pitch limit, radio altitude, and the landing decision height.

Attitude information is provided to the captain and the first officer by the left- and right-side IRS respectively. The centre IRS can be used by either pilot as an alternate source.

The Horizontal Situation Indicator (HSI) presents an electronically generated colour display of navigational data and can show the aircraft's progress on a dynamic map display.

In addition to the EFIS displays, conventional instruments provide ➤➤

The flight deck of a Royal New Zealand Air Force Boeing 757-2K2.
JIM WINCHESTER

The flight engineer's seat and control panel of a Royal New Zealand Air Force Boeing 757-2K2.
JIM WINCHESTER

The left side 'jump' seat of a Royal New Zealand Air Force Boeing 757-2K2.
JIM WINCHESTER

Automatic flight functions manage the aircraft's lateral and vertical flight paths, LNAV and VNAV respectively.

Displays include a map for aircraft orientation and command markers on the airspeed, altitude, and thrust indicators to help pilots fly efficient profiles.

Pilots enter the applicable route and flight data into the CDUs, and the FMS then uses the navigation database, aircraft position and supporting systems to calculate commands for manual and automatic flight path control.

Additionally, the FMS tunes the navigation radios for position updating, and the FMS navigation database supplies the necessary data to fly routes, hold patterns, and procedure turns.

The heart of the flight management system is the flight management computer (FMC). Under normal conditions, one FMC accomplishes the flight management tasks while the other FMC monitors. The second FMC is ready to replace the first FMC if system faults occur.

The FMC uses flight crew–entered flight plan data, aircraft systems data, and data from the navigation database to calculate airplane present position and generate the pitch, roll, and thrust commands necessary to fly an optimum flight profile. Commands are sent by the FMC to the auto-throttle, autopilot, and flight director. Map and route data are sent to the HSIs. The EFIS control panels are used to select the

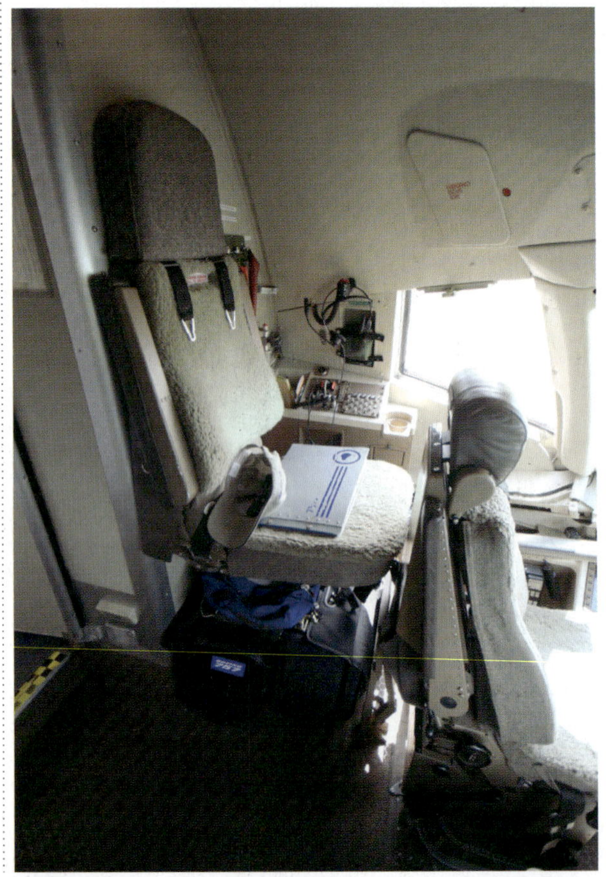

information to aid pilots in controlling the aircraft throughout its flight regime.

A flight recorder provides a permanent record of selected operational systems in a sealed, fire–resistant container. The recorder automatically turns on when either engine is operating, or the aircraft is in flight.

The Boeing 757's air data system consists of the pitot–static system, one temperature probe (TAT), two angle of attack probes, two air data computers (ADCs), and electric flight instruments. The system provides pitot and/or static pressure information to various flight instruments and aircraft systems.

In recent years, many avionics upgrades have been added to the flight deck including larger liquid crystal displays to replace the smaller and older CRTs, satellite communications and an enhanced ground proximity warning system.

Navigation Systems

Navigation systems include the inertial reference system (IRS), global positioning system (GPS), radio navigation systems, weather radar, and the flight management system (FMS).

The IRS calculates aircraft position, acceleration, track, vertical speed, ground speed, true and magnetic heading, wind speed and direction. It also supplies attitude data for the displays, flight management system, flight controls, engine controls, and other systems.

The IRS consists of three inertial reference units and the IRS mode selector panel.

Radio Navigation Systems include a single automatic direction-finding system, two distance measuring equipment systems, two VOR receivers, and three instrument landing system receivers.

Flight Management System

The Boeing 757's FMS aids the flight crew with navigation, in–flight performance optimisation, automatic fuel monitoring, and flight deck displays.

data to be displayed on the HSIs. The mode control panel selects the auto-throttle, autopilot, and flight director operating modes.

The FMC provides navigation guidance and MAP display between 87° north and 87° south latitudes.

Two Control Display Units (CDUs) are used to control the FMC and provide alternate navigation capability if both FMCs fail.

The CDUs can also provide control of other systems which are accessed through the menu page.

The FMC and CDU are used for en route and terminal area navigation, RNAV approaches, and as a supplement to primary navigation means when conducting other types of non-precision approaches.

Automatic Flight Control

The Boeing 757's automatic flight control system consists of the autopilot flight director system and the auto-throttle system. A mode control panel and flight management computer control the AFDS and the auto-throttle system to command the aircraft to perform climb, cruise, descend and approach.

The automatic flight control system (AFDS) consists of three flight control computers (FCCs) and a mode control panel (MCP). The MCP controls the autopilot, flight director, altitude alert, and auto-throttle systems. It also

The flight deck of a Condor Airlines Boeing 757-300.
AIRTEAMIMAGES/MEHRAD WATSON

selects and activates AFDS modes, and establishes altitudes, speeds, and climb/descent profiles.

Three FCCs, located on the left, in the centre, and on the right, control separate hydraulically-powered autopilot control servos to operate flight controls. The autopilot controls ailerons and elevators. Rudder commands are added only during a multiple autopilot approach. Nose wheel steering is also added during rollout from an automatic landing. During an ILS approach with all three autopilots engaged, each ECC is powered by a separate electrical power source. The FCCs also provide inputs for AFDS operating mode displays and flight director commands on the attitude direction indicator (ADI).

The auto-throttle (AT) system provides thrust control from take-off through landing. Auto-throttle mode and speed selection are controlled from the MCP, and the thrust mode select panel (TMSP). When in vertical navigation mode, the FMC selects auto-throttle modes and target thrust values. For example, during final approach flying with a command speed five knots above the landing reference speed at a point 50 feet above the landing threshold dubbed VREF, and landing flaps, there is sufficient wind and gust protection available with the auto-throttle engaged.

The auto-throttle adjusts thrust quickly when the airspeed decreases below the command speed and decreases thrust slowly when the airspeed is above the command speed. In turbulence, the thrust average is higher than necessary to keep the command speed which causes the speed average to be more than the command speed.

The auto-throttle can be operated without using the flight director or the autopilot and can be manually overridden or disconnected by using either of AT disconnect switches.

The thrust management computer (TMC) controls the auto-throttle system through manual inputs from the MCP or automatically from the FMCs while vertical navigation mode is engaged. The basic TMC functions are to:

- Calculate thrust limits and settings or follow FMC thrust settings.
- Detect and transmit auto-throttle failures.
- Actuate the thrust-levers.
- Generate fast slow indications for display on the ADI.

The autopilot and/or flight director can be used after take-off to fly a lateral navigation track and a vertical navigation track provided by the FMC, using both ensures the most economical operation.

SUBSCRIBE TODAY!

WHICH *AIRLINER WORLD* SUBSCRIPTION SUITS YOU BEST?

A 12 MONTH SUBSCRIPTION

BEST VALUE

UK PRINT - 1 year

£59.99

Paying by Annual Direct Debit

2 ISSUES FREE!

B 6 MONTH SUBSCRIPTION

UK PRINT - 6 months

£31.00

Paying by 6-Month Direct Debit

Reader reviews from Pocketmags

REASONS TO SUBSCRIBE TO *AIRLINER WORLD*...

» EXCLUSIVE Subscriber offers on the *Key Publishing* Shop   » SAVE over buying individual issues

» DELIVERED DIRECT to your door   » BE THE FIRST to read the latest features

» SUBSCRIBER DISCOUNTS on *Key Publishing* event tickets

748/25

ENGINES

One Boeing 757 powerplant option was the Rolls-Royce RB211-535E4 engine, each rated at 40,100lb of take-off thrust.

The RB211 engine is a three-rotor axial flow turbofan with high compression and 4.4 bypass ratio. The N1 rotor consists of the fan and a three-stage low-pressure axial flow turbine section on a common shaft and an annular combustion chamber. The N2 rotor consists of a six-stage intermediate pressure axial flow compressor section and a single-stage intermediate pressure axial flow turbine section on a common axial shaft. The N3 rotor consists of a six-stage high-pressure axial flow compressor section and a single-stage high-pressure axial flow turbine section on common shaft. All three rotors are mechanically independent. The N3 rotor drives the engine accessory gearbox.

An RB211-535E4 series engine measures 16ft 6in (5.03m) in length from the front of the nose spinner to the rear of the common nozzle. Its maximum width over the fan casing is 7ft 5in (2.27m) and a height of 7ft 11in (2.41m) from the lowest point on the gearbox to the top face of the engine mount pad. The dry engine weight is 7,600lb (3,449kg) excluding intake, cowls, thrust reverser assembly, exhaust afterbody/jet pipe and nacelle systems.

The engine fuel system automatically controls fuel to maintain a selected engine condition and provides acceleration and deceleration control. The control system senses thrust lever setting, N3, P1, P4 and LP compressor delivery temperature. Fuel is supplied from the aircraft fuel system by a low-pressure fuel pump, through a low-pressure fuel-cooled oil cooler and fuel filter to a high-pressure fuel pump which delivers fuel through a fuel flow governor, flow meter and high-pressure fuel filter and an emergency shut-off valve to a fuel manifold and fuel spray nozzles located in the combustion section of the engine. Manual control of the fuel flow for engine starting and stopping is effected through a three-position fuel switch controlling the electrical supply to a shut-off valve and a fuel enrichment valve solenoid.

Each engine has individual flight deck controls. Thrust is set by positioning the thrust levers which are positioned automatically by the auto-throttle system or manually by the flight crew.

Each engine is controlled by an electronic engine controller (EEC) which monitors auto-throttle and flight crew inputs through the thrust levers to automatically control the engines. »

Delta Air Lines once operated a fleet of 177 Boeing 757s powered by Pratt & Whitney PW2037 turbofan engines.
AIRTEAMIMAGES/ALEX PEAKE

Close-up shot of a Rolls-Royce RB211-535E4-series engine. AIRTEAMIMAGES

Engine indications are displayed on the engine indication and crew alerting system (EICAS) display.

Engine Pressure Ratio is the primary thrust parameter with the following associated annunciations:

- Maximum EPR
- Thrust Reference Mode
- Reference/Target EPR indication
- Reference EPR
- Assumed Temperature
- Thrust Reverser Indication
- Command Thrust Level
- Commanded EPR Sector

Maximum EPR is the maximum certified thrust limit for all phases of flight and varies with existing ambient conditions. The maximum EPR is indicated by dual amber radials on the periphery of the EPR indicator.

With the EEC ON, the thrust levers can be moved to the forward stop and the engines will not exceed the displayed maximum EPR.

The thrust management computer calculates a reference EPR based on existing pressure altitude and ambient temperature data from the air data system for the following modes:

- TO   Take-off
- TO1   Take-off one
- TO2   Take-off two
- D-TO   Assumed temperature take-off

Cutaway of the Rolls-Royce RB211-535E4-series engine. ROLLS-ROYCE

- CLB   Climb
- CLB1 Climb one
- CLB2 Climb two
- CRZ   Cruise
- CON   Continuous
- GA   Go-around

Any mode can be selected with the thrust mode select panel (TMSP).

Two levels of reduced take-off thrust are available with the 1 and 2 mode switches on the TMSP. These are lower thrust ratings than take-off thrust. Measured against take-off thrust, TO1 is approximately 88% and TO2 is approximately 80%.

Electronic Engine Control

The thrust system consists of a hydromechanical engine fuel control with an electronic engine control (EEC) unit. The EEC sets thrust by controlling EPR based on thrust lever position. EPR is commanded by positioning the thrust levers either automatically with the auto-throttles, or manually by the flight crew. Both engines may be operated by conventional hydromechanical control by disengaging the EECs. Each engine EEC is powered by dual dedicated generators and continuously compute the maximum limits for thrust.

Maximum rated thrust is available in any phase of flight by moving the thrust levers to the full forward positions. Maximum EPR represents the maximum rated thrust available from the engine. These values are displayed by the position of the amber radial on the EPR display. If the EEC fails or is turned off, the values are computed by the TMC and displayed in the same manner. If the TMC fails, the maximum limits are blank.

During normal EEC operation, each EEC provides a trim input to its associated hydromechanical fuel controller to drive the engine to an EEC-computed command thrust level. The EEC computes this EPR as a percentage of its maximum limit computation. The percentage is varied with thrust lever position, such that at full throttle, the percentage is 100%. During rapid throttle lever movements, the difference between the engines actual EPR and the EEC-commanded EPR is displayed as the command sector on the EICAS EPR display. The engine is controlled by its hydromechanical fuel controls at low power operating conditions.

The RB211 has two idle speeds, minimum and approach. The fuel control unit selects idle speeds automatically. Minimum idle is a lower thrust than approach idle and is selected for ground operation and all phases of flight except approach and landing. Approach idle is selected whenever this higher idle setting is required for proper system operation.

The thrust control system also includes an electronic engine limiter control (ELC) unit. If required, both engines may be operated conventionally by manually »

Close-up shot of a Pratt & Whitney PW2000-series engine. PRATT & WHITNEY

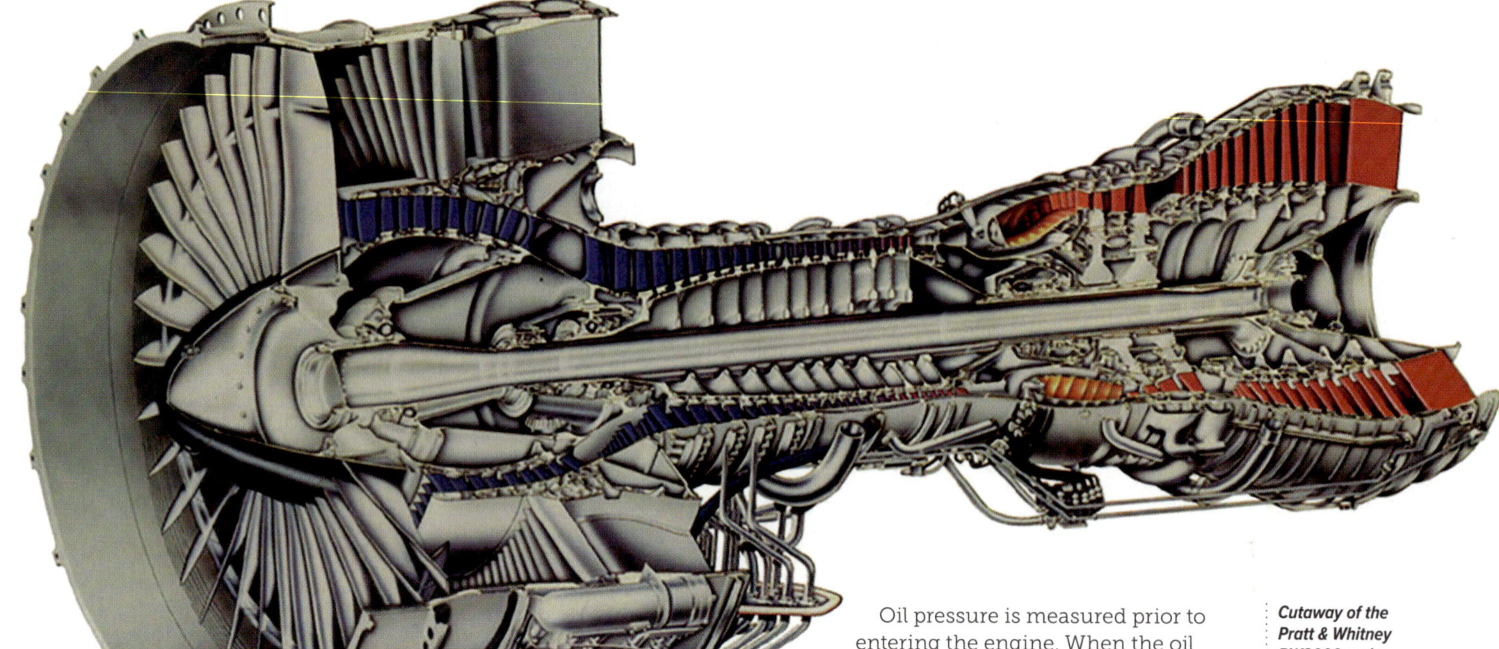

Cutaway of the Pratt & Whitney PW2000-series engine. PRATT & WHITNEY

disengaging the ELCs. Each engine ELC is powered by dual dedicated generators.

Air from the pneumatic duct is used to power the air driven starter, which is connected to the N3 rotor (the N2 rotor on the PW2037). The starter air source may be a ground cart, the APU, or the other running engine.

The ENG START selectors control the start valves. Ignition and fuel flow are controlled through the FUEL CONTROL switches.

Engine Fuel System

Fuel is supplied by pumps located in the tanks. The fuel flows through a spar fuel valve located in the main tank. It then passes through the first stage engine fuel pump where additional pressure is added. It flows through a fuel/oil heat exchanger where it is pre-heated, and a filter removes contaminants. The second stage of the engine fuel pump adds more pressure before the fuel reaches the fuel control unit, which adjusts fuel flow to meet thrust requirements. The fuel then flows through the engine fuel valve, fuel flow meter and a second fuel filter before entering the engine.

On the PW2037 the fuel is controlled to meet the existing thrust requirements and then flows through the engine fuel valve and fuel flow meter before entering the engine.

The engine fuel control system incorporates a hydromechanical fuel control unit which operates in conjunction with the EEC and ELC units. The fuel control system schedules fuel flow to meet engine thrust requirements as dictated by the thrust lever position and the specific engine operating conditions. The EEC trims the metered fuel to prevent over boost when operating at or near the thrust limits and the ELC trims the metered fuel to prevent N1 from exceeding the limits.

The oil system provides pressurised oil to lubricate and cool the engine main bearings, gears, accessory drives, and provides automatic fuel heating for fuel system icing protection.

Oil is pressurised by a main (engine-driven) pump. From the pump, the oil flows through the main oil filter where contaminants are removed. The main oil filter cannot be bypassed. The LEFT or RIGHT OIL FILTER EICAS advisory message displays to indicate the main oil filter is clogged.

The oil flows through the oil cooler, and is then delivered to the engine main bearings, gears, and accessory drives. A scavenge pump returns the oil to the reservoir. Prior to the reservoir, the oil flows through a scavenge oil filter. If the scavenge oil filter becomes clogged, then oil bypasses the filter.

Oil pressure, temperature, and quantity are displayed on the secondary engine display.

Oil pressure is measured prior to entering the engine. When the oil pressure is at or below the variable limits, the EICAS indication changes to amber.

The LEFT or RIGHT ENG OIL PRESS light illuminates and the LEFT or RIGHT ENG OIL PRESS EICAS advisory message displays to indicate the oil pressure is low.

Oil temperature is measured after leaving the engine, prior to entering the reservoir.

There is no minimum oil quantity limit (no amber or red line limit) and there are no operating limitations for the engine oil quantity; therefore, there are no flight crew procedures based solely on a response to low oil quantity.

Thrust Reverser System

Each engine has a hydraulically actuated fan air thrust reverser. Reverse thrust is available only on the ground.

Reverse thrust levers can be raised only when the forward thrust levers are in the idle position. An interlock stop limits thrust to idle reverse while the reverser is in transit and the EECs control thrust limits during reverse operation. When the reverse-thrust levers are pulled aft to the interlock position the auto-throttle disengages and the auto-speed brakes deploy.

When the reverser system is activated:

- Reverser isolation valve opens allowing the reverser translating sleeves to hydraulically move aft.
- The fan flow blocker doors rotate into place to direct fan air through stationary cascade guide vanes.
- The reverser indication (REV) is displayed above each digital EPR indication (REV is displayed in amber when the reverser is in transit).

When the interlock releases:

- The reverse thrust levers can be raised to the maximum reverse thrust position.
- The REV indication changes to green when the reverser is fully deployed.

Pushing the reverse thrust levers to the fully down position retracts the reversers to the stowed and locked position. While the reverser is in transit, the REV annunciation changes colour to amber. The thrust levers cannot be moved forward until the reverse thrust levers are fully down. When the reverser reaches the stowed position, the amber REV annunciation disappears.

Pratt & Whitney PW2037 Engine System

Another Boeing 757 powerplant option was the Pratt and Whitney PW2037 engine, each rated at 37,000lb of take-off thrust.

The engines are two–rotor axial flow turbofans of high compression and bypass ratio. The N1 rotor consists of the fan, a low-pressure compressor and turbine section on a common shaft. The N2 rotor consists of a high-pressure compressor and turbine section on a common shaft. The N1 and N2 rotors are mechanically independent. The N2

A Pratt & Whitney PW2037 engine during maintenance.
DELTA TECHOPS

rotor drives the engine accessory gearbox.

A PW2000 series engine measures 12ft 2in (3.73m) in length, and 7ft (2.16m) wide. The dry engine weight including all essential accessories necessary for engine operation, but excluding starter, exhaust nozzle, and power

source for the ignition system is 7,300lb (3,311kg).

Each engine has individual flight deck controls. Thrust is set by positioning the thrust levers which are positioned automatically by the auto-throttle system or manually by the flight crew.

Each engine is controlled by an electronic engine controller (EEC) which monitors auto-throttle and flight crew inputs through the thrust levers to automatically control the engines.

Engine indications are displayed on the engine indication and crew alerting system (EICAS) display.

Many of the sub-systems on the PW2037 function in the same way as those on

the Rolls-Royce RB211-535, those that differ are listed.

Electronic Engine Control

The thrust system consists of a dual channel (primary and secondary), full authority electronic engine control unit without any hydromechanical backup. The EEC sets thrust by controlling EPR based on thrust lever position. EPR is commanded by positioning the thrust levers either automatically with the auto-throttles, or manually by the flight crew. Each EEC is powered, when the engines are operating, by a dedicated permanent magnet alternator (PMA) which is independent of aircraft electrical power.

The EEC continuously computes the maximum limits for thrust. Maximum rated thrust is available in any phase of flight by moving the thrust levers to the full forward positions. Maximum EPR represents the maximum rated thrust available from the engine. These values are displayed by the position of the dual amber radials on the EPR display.

An American Airlines Boeing 757-200 seen on take-off from New York-JFK powered by Rolls-Royce RB211-535E4 engines.
AIRTEAMIMAGES/VINCENZO PACE

During normal EEC operation, the primary channel provides inputs to the fuel control to drive the engine to an EEC computed command thrust level. The EEC computes this EPR as a percentage of its maximum limit computation. The percentage is varied with thrust lever position, such that at full throttle, the percentage is 100%. During rapid throttle lever movements, the difference between the engines actual EPR and the EECs commanded EPR is displayed as the command sector on the EICAS EPR display.

The PW2037 engine has three idle speeds: ground minimum idle, inflight minimum idle and approach idle. The fuel control unit selects these idle speeds automatically. Ground minimum idle is a lower thrust than inflight minimum idle and selected for ground operations. Inflight minimum idle is a lower thrust than approach idle and is for most phases of flight. Approach idle is selected whenever this higher idle setting is required for proper system operation.

The engine fuel control system incorporates a fuel control unit which operates in conjunction with the EEC. The fuel control system schedules fuel flow to meet engine thrust requirements as dictated by the thrust lever position and the specific engine operating conditions. The EEC controls the metered fuel and prevents engine limits from being exceeded.

Engine Oil System

As a PW2037 engine is started, a quantity of oil will shift to the engine bearing compartments and gearbox and will not return to the oil reservoir until the engine is shut down. In addition, oil quantity and oil temperature will tend to vary with engine RPM such that, as RPM is increased, quantity and temperature increase. As RPM is decreased, quantity and temperature decrease.

Oil is pressurised by a main (engine–driven) oil pump. From the pump, the oil flows through the oil filter where contaminants are removed. Should the oil filter become saturated with contaminants, oil will automatically bypass the filter. The EICAS advisory message LEFT or RIGHT OIL FILTER displays indicating the oil filter is bypassed. The oil flows through the fuel-oil heat exchanger where fuel is used as the heat sink, and is then delivered to the engine main bearings, gears, and accessory drives. The oil is then returned to the reservoir.

APU System

The auxiliary power unit (APU) is a self–contained gas turbine engine located in the aircraft's tail cone. The APU air inlet door is located between the horizontal and vertical stabilisers on the right side of the aircraft.

While the primary purpose of the APU is to supply electrical power and bleed air on the ground before engine start, the APU can also be started inflight, and operated up to the aircraft's maximum certified altitude.

Electrical power has priority over bleed air. Electrical power is available throughout the aircraft operating envelope. In flight, APU bleed air is available up to an altitude of approximately 17,000ft.

Landing
Gears

A Boeing 757 has two main landing gears and a single nose gear. Each main gear has four wheels in tandem pairs and the nose gear is a conventional steerable two–wheel unit.

Hydraulic power for retraction, extension, and steering is supplied by the left hydraulic system. An alternate extension system is also provided.

The normal/reserve brake hydraulic system is powered by the aircraft's right side hydraulic system and the alternate brake hydraulic system is powered by the aircraft's left side hydraulic system.

Both systems have anti-skid protection, though the autobrake system is only available through the normal system.

Air and Ground Sensing System

In–flight and ground operation of various aircraft systems are controlled by two sensing systems.

An air and ground (A/G) sensing system receives logic signals from tilt sensors located on each main landing gear which configure aircraft systems to the appropriate air or ground status.

A nose A/G sensing system receives logic signals from nose gear strut compression sensors which control stall warning and portions of the caution and warning system.

Landing Gear Operation

A Boeing 757's landing gear is normally controlled by the landing

The arrangement of a Boeing 757's landing gears are clearly shown in this landing shot of a Jet2 aircraft. AIRTEAMIMAGES/ ENDA BURKE

gear lever. On the ground, the lever is prevented from moving to its UP position by an automatic lever lock controlled by the main gear tilt sensors. When the gear is not tilted (when the aircraft is on the ground) the lock is engaged. The lever lock can be manually overridden by pushing and holding the landing gear lever lock override switch.

In flight, the lever lock is automatically released through A/G sensing of the main gear tilt sensor.

Retraction

After take-off both main landing gears tilt, releasing the lever lock. When the landing gear lever is positioned to UP, the landing gear begins to retract. The gear down green lights extinguish, the GEAR and DOORS lights illuminate showing gear is in transit (gear, doors and lever position disagree).

The landing gear doors open, and the tilted main gear and nose gear move to the retract position.

Automatic wheel braking occurs during gear retraction.

After retraction, all three landing gears and their doors are held up by uplocks. The GEAR and DOORS lights extinguish. The landing gear lever is placed in the OFF position to depressurise the landing gear system.

The GEAR light remains illuminated, and the EICAS caution message GEAR DISAGREE display if any gear is not up and locked up after the normal transit time. The affected gear's, gear »

A close-up photo of the left side 757 main landing gear. NASA

down light, remains illuminated if the gear never unlocked from the down position. The DOORS light remains illuminated, and the EICAS advisory message GEAR DOORS display if any hydraulically actuated door is not closed after normal transit time.

EICAS denotes Engine Indicating and Crew Alerting System.

Extension

When the landing gear lever is moved to DOWN, the landing gear doors open, the gears are unlocked, and the GEAR and DOORS lights illuminate.

The gears are hydraulically powered to the down and locked position. The down locks are powered to the locked position, all hydraulically actuated gear doors close, and the main gear trucks hydraulically tilt to the flight position. When all gears are down and locked, the gear down lights illuminate and the GEAR and DOORS lights extinguish.

The GEAR light remains illuminated, and the EICAS caution message GEAR DISAGREE display if any gear is not locked down after the normal transit time. The extinguished gear down light indicates the affected gear. The DOORS light remains illuminated, and the EICAS advisory message GEAR DOORS display if any hydraulically actuated door is not closed after the normal transit time.

Alternate Extension

The Boeing 757's alternate landing gear extension system uses a dedicated DC powered electric hydraulic pump. Fluid within the supply line to the pump is sufficient for alternate gear extension operation. This fluid is isolated from the left hydraulic system. Selecting the ALTN GEAR EXTEND switch releases all door and gear

uplocks. The landing gears free–fall to the down and locked position.

When all gears are down and locked, the gear down lights illuminate and the GEAR light extinguishes. During alternate extension, the DOORS light remains illuminated, and the EICAS advisory message GEAR DOORS display because all the hydraulically powered gear doors remain open.

Nose Wheel Steering

Nose wheel steering is powered by the aircraft's left side hydraulic system.

Primary steering control is provided by the left sidewall nose wheel steering tiller. Limited steering control is available through the rudder pedals. The tiller can turn the nose wheel up to 65° in either direction. A pointer on the tiller assembly shows the tiller's position relative to the neutral setting. The rudder pedals can be used to turn the nose wheels up to 7° in either direction. Tiller inputs override rudder pedal inputs.

Brake System

Each main gear wheel has a multiple disc brake. The nose wheels have no brakes. The brake system includes:

- Normal/reserve brake hydraulic system.
- Alternate brake hydraulic system.
- Brake accumulator.
- Anti-skid protection.
- Auto-brake system.
- Parking brake.

Normal Brake Hydraulic System

Powered by the aircraft's right side hydraulic system. The brake pedals provide independent control of the left and right brakes.

The right-side main landing gear during a functional retraction test. UNITED AIRLINES

The 757's nose gear comprises a conventional steerable two–wheel unit.

Alternate Brake Hydraulic System

Selection is automatic. If the aircraft's right side hydraulic system pressure is low, the left side hydraulic system automatically supplies pressure to the alternate brake system. Pushing a brake pedal then sends hydraulic pressure through the alternate antiskid valves to the brakes.

The BRAKE SOURCE light illuminates and the EICAS advisory message BRAKE SOURCE displays if both the normal and the alternate brake system pressures are low.

Parking Brake

The parking brake can be set with the normal/reserve or alternate brake hydraulic system. If either of the systems are not pressurised, parking brake pressure is maintained by the brake accumulator which is pressurised by the aircraft's right side hydraulic system. Accumulator pressure is shown on the BRAKE PRESS indicator.

The parking brake is set by fully depressing both brake pedals, pulling the parking brake handle up, then releasing the pedals. This mechanically latches the pedals in the depressed position and commands the parking brake valve to close. The parking brake is released by depressing the pedals until the parking brake handle releases.

THE DESTINATION FOR
AVIATION ENTHUSIASTS

Visit us today and discover all our latest releases

Order today from our online shop...

keybooks.co.uk

Call +44 (0)1780 480404 *(Monday to Friday 9am - 5.30pm GMT)*

**Free 2nd class P&P on BFPO orders. Overseas charges apply.*

795/25

Flight **Controls**

A Boeing 757's primary flight controls are elevators, ailerons, and rudders which are controlled by the control column, control wheel, and rudder pedals.

Primary flight controls are powered by redundant hydraulic systems with no manual reversion. Secondary flight controls include a moveable horizontal stabiliser, spoilers, and leading and trailing edge flaps. Spoilers operate differentially to assist ailerons for roll control and symmetrically as speed brakes.

Three guarded flight control shutoff switches control hydraulic power to the stabiliser, elevators, and rudder.

Pilot controls consist of:

- Two control columns
- Two control wheels
- Two pairs of rudder pedals

- Control wheel stabiliser trim switches
- The speed brake lever allows manual or automatic symmetric actuation of the spoilers.
- The flap lever
- Aileron trim switches
- Rudder trim switch
- Alternate stabiliser trim switches

The columns and wheels are connected through jam override

mechanisms. If a jam occurs in a column or wheel, the pilots can maintain control by applying force to the other column or wheel to overcome the jam. When a restricted portion of the flight controls are bypassed, some control effectiveness may be lost.

Pitch Control

Pitch control is provided by two elevators and a movable horizontal stabiliser. A Mach speed trim system operates the stabiliser to improve speed stability.

Moving the control column signals hydraulic actuators to move the elevators. Elevator positions are shown on the EICAS status display. Separate pointers indicate the

Flaps and spoilers extended on a Britannia Airways Boeing 757 during maintenance at Luton Airport. AIRTEAMIMAGES/ DEREK PEDLEY

left and right elevator deflection. A full–scale indication corresponds to the maximum elevator deflection.

If one control column should jam, applying significant forward or aft force to the other causes the two columns to override. Pitch control is then available using the free control column path.

Two elevator feel systems provide artificial feel forces to the pilots control columns. Mechanical springs provide feel following a loss of the aircraft's centre and right-side hydraulic systems.

The horizontal stabiliser is powered by the centre and right hydraulic systems. Stabiliser position commands are sent to the stabiliser trim control modules, one for each stabiliser hydraulic source, which control hydraulic power to the stabiliser.

Stabiliser position is displayed on two indicators located on the control stand. Green bands indicate the normal trim settings for take-off.

Stabiliser trim control has three modes: electric, alternate, and automatic.

Dual electric pitch trim switches located on the control wheel must be pushed simultaneously to command trim changes.

Alternate trim control is provided by the alternate stabiliser trim switches on the control stand. Pushing both switches simultaneously commands trim changes and provides an increased range of stabiliser travel.

Roll Control

Roll control is provided by two ailerons and ten spoilers.

An aileron is located on each wing on either side of the outboard trailing edge flap. Aileron surface deflections are proportional to control wheel displacement. Spoilers begin to extend to augment roll control after several degrees of control wheel rotation.

The control wheels are connected so that, if one jams, using significant force causes the control wheels to override. Roll control is then available using the free control wheel.

Aileron positions are shown on the EICAS status display where a full–scale indication corresponds to maximum aileron deflection.

Dual aileron trim switches located on the aft aisle stand must be pushed simultaneously to command trim changes. Hydraulic power from one of the three hydraulic systems is necessary to accurately set aileron trim. The amount of aileron trim is indicated on a scale on the top of each control column.

Yaw Control

Yaw control is provided by a single rudder and two yaw dampers operate through the rudder control system to improve directional stability.

Rudder position is shown on the EICAS status display. On the ground, a full-scale indication corresponds to the maximum rudder deflection.

Rudder trim control can be used to command trim changes.

The stabiliser is controlled automatically by the autopilot or by a Mach speed trim system when the autopilots are not engaged. The Mach speed trim system improves speed stability by trimming the stabiliser as airspeed changes.

Automatic stabiliser trim uses only one trim control module and trims at one-half the electric or alternate trim rate.

Control commands from the rudder pedals and trim control are modified by a rudder ratio changer. As airspeed increases the ratio changer desensitizes these commands from the pilot to reduce the rudder deflection.

The ratio changer receives air data computer airspeed inputs and provides control commands to an actuator powered by the aircraft's left side hydraulic system. The actuator then dampens the pilot's inputs to the rudder.

Additionally, yaw damper systems improve turn coordination and Dutch roll damping.

Spoilers

Six spoiler panels are located on the upper surface of each wing. Spoilers on opposing wings are symmetrically paired.

Spoiler panels are used as speed brakes to increase drag and reduce lift, both in flight and on the ground. The spoilers also supplement roll control in response to control wheel commands.

Flaps and Slats

The trailing edge flaps and leading-edge slats are high lift devices that increase wing lift and decrease stall speed during take-off, approach, and landing.

Flap and slat positions are indicated by two pointers in the flap position indicator. There are left and right pointers for the left- and right-wing flaps and slats.

Flap positions 1, 5, 15, 20 are for take-off, while positions 25 and 30 are for landing, and position 20 is used for some non-normal landing conditions.

A flap load relief system protects the flaps from excessive air loads so if the flap airspeed placard limit is exceeded with the flaps in position 30, the flaps automatically retract to position 25. When airspeed is reduced, the flaps automatically re–extend.

Electrical, Hydraulic and Fuel Systems

The Boeing 757's electrical system generates and distributes AC and DC power to other aircraft systems, and is comprised of main AC power, main DC power, battery/standby power, and the hydraulic driven generator. System operation is automatic, and electrical faults are automatically detected and isolated.

The AC electrical system is the main source for aircraft electrical power and the entire aircraft's AC electrical load can be supplied by any two main AC power sources: either the left or right integrated drive generator or the APU generator.

The aircraft's entire AC electrical load can also be supplied by external power sources isolated from one another.

Each engine has an IDG with automatic control and system protection functions. When an engine starts, with the GENERATOR CONTROL switch selected ON, the IDG automatically powers the respective main bus, and the previous power source is disconnected from that bus.

The IDG can be electrically disconnected from the busses by pushing the GEN CTRL switch to OFF and can also be electrically disconnected from its respective bus by selecting external power prior to engine shutdown.

The OFF light in the GEN CTRL switch illuminates, and the EICAS Advisory message LEFT or RIGHT GEN OFF displays whenever the generator control breaker is open.

The DRIVE light illuminates and the EICAS advisory message LEFT or RIGHT GEN DRIVE displays when low oil pressure or high oil temperature is

The hydraulic driven generator (HDG) activates automatically when both the left and right main AC busses are unpowered and is powered by the aircraft's left side hydraulic system.

The HDG provides AC power to the left, right and standby AC transfer busses, the captain's flight instrument transfer bus, it also provides DC power to the hot battery, battery, and standby DC busses.

The amount of DC power produced by the HDG is less than the DC power produced by a fully charged battery. When the HDG first begins to operate, the battery DISCH light may illuminate until the battery power decreases to the power level produced by the HDG.

Hydraulics System

A Boeing 757 has three independent hydraulic systems: left, right, and centre, which power the flight controls, leading edge slats, trailing edge flaps, landing gear, wheel brakes, nose wheel steering, thrust reversers, and autopilot servos.

The flight control system's components are distributed so that any one hydraulic system can provide adequate aircraft controllability.

The aircraft's left side hydraulic system powers flight controls, flaps and slats, landing gear, alternate brakes, nose wheel steering, left engine thrust reverser and the hydraulic driven generator.

The aircraft's right side hydraulic system (which is like the left side system) consists of a reservoir, engine–driven pump, and an electric motor–driven pump. It powers the flight controls, normal brakes, reserve brakes, right engine thrust reverser, and the PTU.

Both the left and right-side systems consist of a reservoir, and an identical engine–driven pump, electric motor–driven pump, and a power transfer unit (PTU) pump.

The centre system only powers flight controls and consists of a reservoir (like the left side reservoir), two electric motor–driven pumps (like the left side system), and a ram air turbine (RAT) pump. The reservoir maintains reserve hydraulic fluid for use by the RAT in the event of a centre system hydraulic leak.

When deployed, the RAT provides hydraulic power to the flight controls portion of the centre hydraulic system, and adequate hydraulic power at speeds above 130kts. In flight, the RAT deploys automatically if both engines fail.

Hydraulic fluid is supplied to each hydraulic pump from the associated system reservoir which are pressurised by the bleed air system.

The right-side reservoir maintains a reserve hydraulic fluid for use by the reserve brakes in the event of a right system hydraulic leak.

A quantity measuring system provides information to the EICAS status display.

The reservoir maintains reserve hydraulic fluid for use by the PTU in the event of a left system hydraulic leak.

Fluid for the engine–driven pump (the primary pump) flows through a shut-off valve controlled by the engine fire switch. Pulling the fire switch shuts off the flow of fluid to the engine pump and depressurises the pump.

The PTU is a hydraulic motor pump which transfers hydraulic power from the right system to the left system. The PTU is automatically activated if the left engine–driven pump fails or the left engine–driven pump pressure is low. When activated, the PTU supplements the left side electric motor–driven pump to operate the flaps and slats, landing gear, nose wheel steering, and hydraulic driven generator.

PTU operation is inhibited if the right engine is not operating.

Fuel System

The Boeing 757's fuel system supplies fuel to the engines and the APU. The fuel is contained in three tanks, a centre tank and left and right main tanks.

Fuel quantity data, measured by probes in each tank, is fed to the fuel quantity processor where it is corrected for density then displayed on a fuel quantity indicator for each tank.

When total usable fuel in either the left or right main tank drops below approximately 2,200lb, the FUEL CONFIG light illuminates and the LOW FUEL caution message is displayed.

Each fuel tank contains two AC–powered pumps. A single pump can supply sufficient fuel to operate one engine under all conditions.

The two centre tank fuel pumps have greater output pressure than the left and right main tank fuel pumps. When all six pumps are operating, the centre tank pumps override the left and right main tank pumps so that centre tank fuel is used before left or right main tank fuel.

The fuel manifolds are arranged so that any fuel tank pump can supply either engine. Two cross-feed valves isolate the left fuel manifold from the right. These valves are normally closed providing fuel feed from tank to engine. Both valves are opened any time it becomes necessary to feed an engine from an opposite fuel tank. Only one open cross-feed valve is required for successful cross-feed operation.

A VALVE disagreement light illuminates and the EICAS advisory message FWD FUEL X–FEED or AFT FUEL X–FEED displays if a valve position does not agree with its switch position. With either cross-feed valve open, the LEFT or RIGHT FUEL SYS PRESS messages are inhibited.

Fuel is supplied to the APU from the left fuel manifold.

Ground fuelling underway of an Air Astana Boeing 757-200 at Frankfurt Airport, Germany.
AIRTEAMIMAGES/RALF MAYERMANN

detected in an IDG. The IDG drive can be disconnected from the engine by pushing the respective DRIVE DISC switch. The IDG cannot be reconnected by the flight crew.

The main DC electrical system uses transformer–rectifier units (TRUs) to produce DC power. The TRUs are powered by the main AC busses. The TRUs operate isolated from one another. If one TRU fails, the DC bus tie breaker closes (when both BUS TIE switches are in AUTO) to keep both DC busses powered. There are no flight deck controls for the main DC electrical system.

The battery/standby power electrical system can supply DC and AC power to selected flight instruments, communications and navigation systems, and other critical systems, if there are main AC and DC electrical power system failures.

The battery/standby power system consists of a hot battery bus, a battery bus, a standby DC bus, and a standby AC bus.

ARIES
NASA's Transport Testbed

David Willis details the life of the National Aeronautics and Space Administration's (NASA) Boeing 757 and highlights some of the many research programmes it participated in during its career as a testbed.

Although several Boeing 757s have been involved in NASA projects, the Administration has only ever owned one example of the airliner. Between 1994 and 2009 a Boeing 757 aircraft served as a research platform with the organisation, primarily tasked with evaluating technology with the aim of improving aviation safety. Several of the systems it pioneered have since become common in commercial aviation today.

Transport Systems Research Vehicle

Until 1997, NASA's primary commercial aircraft research platform was Boeing 737-130 N515NA (c/n 19437), the first 737 built. NASA modified the 737 as its Transport Systems Research Vehicle to conduct trials of equipment and techniques of interest to both industry and the airlines. Among the many changes installed was a second cockpit in the forward cabin, which helped develop and demonstrate technology used in the electronic flight displays that later became standard in the Boeing 757 and Boeing 767.

The aircraft had joined NASA on May 17, 1974, with a total of 978 flight hours, adding just over 2,000 more in its first 20 years with the Administration. By the time it was retired, the 737 was no longer typical of many airliners in service, as technology had moved on considerably in the 30 years since it first flew. Its cockpit was analogue at a time when electronic flight instrumentation was becoming standard, while the cost of supporting the aircraft in service increased as it aged. Space in the aircraft's cabin was also limited and in the early 1990s, NASA began looking for a replacement aircraft.

Boeing 757

On March 24, 1994, the Administration acquired Boeing 757-225 (c/n 22191) from the defunct Eastern Air Lines for $24m. The aircraft was the second of its kind built and the first delivered to an airline, and joined Eastern as N501EA in August 1983. It had been stored at McCarran International Airport in Las Vegas, Nevada, since January 1991, when the carrier ceased operations. As well as having a larger cabin than the 737 the aircraft was more representative of the modern airliner, with a two-person cockpit and modern electronic cockpit systems. It was powered by Rolls-Royce RB511-535E4 engines, far more fuel efficient and quieter than the Pratt & Whitney JT8Ds of NASA's 737-130.

The jet was delivered to the Langley Research Center in Hampton, Virginia, on May 19, 1994. Re-registered as N557NA, its former airline titles along the top of the cabin were replaced with Langley Research Center, although it retained the basic scheme it had worn in commercial service. It was only in late 1999 that the 757 was repainted in the traditional NASA house colour scheme, with white uppers and a blue cheatline on the fuselage and NASA 557 carried on the tail.

Modifications

Following a short series of familiarisation flights from Hampton, the aircraft was slightly modified to participate in the High Intensity Radiated Field programme, which investigated the electromagnetic environment in and around aircraft, after which more extensive changes were planned. The airliner had been acquired to serve as the airborne component of the Transport Research Facilities (TRF), a diverse set of tools to develop and test new technology concepts to enhance the capacity, safety, and operational needs of the US national airspace system using the simulation-to-flight concept.

In addition to the 757, TRF comprised a range of ground-based facilities, including various cockpit simulators within the Cockpit Motion Facility (CMF). CMF contained the integration flight deck, which resembled the 757 cockpit; the research flight deck was used for crew workload and systems integration work; and the Research System Integration Laboratory (RSIL), which replicated the Transport Research System (TRS) installed in the 757's cabin. RSIL's function was to simulate the integration of key hardware and software in the aircraft. The second facility was the Flight System Integration Laboratory, used for aircraft integration and preflight validation of the hardware and software due to be installed in the 757.

Prior to entering service with NASA, the aircraft was modified to enhance its value as a research tool. The TRS was the basic experimental infrastructure installed in the aircraft – the computers, data recording systems and other hardware that allow tests to be conducted and monitored. The cabin was configured to allow 14 test pallets/ research workstations to be carried as its baseline layout, although provision for six more positions was provided should they be required for specific research tasks. A video recorder was mounted on the tail to record the forward view and observe the control surfaces on the wings in flight, while other cameras could be mounted on the exterior or interior of the aircraft to cover areas of interest. All video feed could be recorded for later analysis, along with various flight parameters. TRS first became operational in June 1997 and was upgraded as the Uncoupled Baseline TRS in December 1998. During that month the aircraft was christened the Airborne Research Integrated Experiments System, ARIES for short. »

NASA's Boeing 757 was operated by the Administration for 15 years before budget cuts resulted in it being withdrawn. *NASA*

ARIES was repainted in NASA livery during 1999. The aircraft was extensively modified as an experimental testbed, although external changes were minimal. *NASA*

Original plans to install a second cockpit in the cabin, as in the 737-130, were thwarted by a shortage of funds. Instead, the left side of the flight deck was modified as the Flight Deck Research Station (FDRS) to allow the evaluation of flight systems and operational procedures. The jump seat position was configured for a second safety pilot, while a fourth place in the cockpit was added for an observer. The Uncoupled Baseline TRS was linked to the FDRS, allowing guidance from the test personnel in the cabin to be displayed at the cockpit test station. Data generated in the FDRS could also be recorded and observed by the TRS mounted in the cabin. A later modification to the TRS, known as the Coupled Baseline configuration, permitted the aircraft to be flown by systems mounted in the cabin, while the pilots in the cockpit monitored for safety. It was first used in August 1999.

Research Projects

ARIES became a vital research tool for NASA's Airframe Systems, Aviation Safety and Aviation Systems Capacity programmes. Over the years it participated in a number of diverse trials, including low visibility landing and surface operations in 1997, which evolved into the Runway Incursion Prevention System, during which the aircraft operated at Dallas-Fort Worth Airport, Texas, in 2000. The Runway Winter Operations project measured runway friction when icing, snow and water were present, the data generated being used to create an index to standardise reporting of such conditions.

During 1999 NASA teamed with Honeywell for the Airborne Information for Lateral Spacing trials to improve safety at airports with parallel runways. The aim was to reduce minimum runway separation in low visibility from the then mandated 4,300ft (1,311m), so that closer parallel runways could continue to operate when weather conditions meant pilots could no longer see aircraft landing or taking-off next to them. The 757 was equipped with experimental systems to increase positional accuracy, conducting flight trails at NASA Wallops Flight Facility in Virginia alongside Honeywell's Gulfstream IV. During November 1999 the capability was demonstrated to Federal Aviation Administration officials at Minneapolis-St Paul International Airport, Minnesota.

Other projects that the 757 participated in included the use of the global positioning system (GPS) satellite constellation to help automate landings and, from 2000, trials to develop synthetic vision systems. During 2004, ARIES tested a radar system able to detect turbulence by measuring the motion of moisture in the air. Although the aircraft was primarily used as a test platform for new technology, it also took part in studies of jet-engine contrails to determine their effects on the atmosphere.

Retirement

Although ARIES had proved its worth over the years, its future became increasingly uncertain as NASA's budget declined sharply during the first decade of the 21st century. Cuts had to be made. Although it was originally expected that ARIES would remain in service for at least 20 years, the Administration reluctantly decided to place the aircraft into flyable storage towards the end of the decade. During the last week of January 2009 the Boeing 757 departed Langley for the last time, initially for the Dryden Flight Research Center at Edwards Air Force Base, California. The period of storage was short, however, for in April the Boeing 757 was sold to L-3 Capital via Starflite International Corp, becoming N144DC. It remains registered to L-3 Capital today.

Losing ARIES deprived NASA of a valuable tool in its pursuit of making commercial airliner operations safer. While the Administration has been involved in projects that made temporary use of other Boeing 757s – such as the ecoDemonstrator – no other examples of the airliner have flown in its distinctive colours.

While ARIES was the only Boeing 757 owned by NASA, other examples of the type have been used in projects involving the Administration, including a Boeing ecoDemonstrator.
NASA

Catfish

Forty years after its maiden flight, the first Boeing 757 continues to earn its keep. For most of its existence the aircraft has played a significant role supporting the Lockheed Martin F-22 Raptor fighter. **David Willis** details the career of the aircraft – unofficially dubbed the Catfish.

The first Boeing 757 after modification as the Avionics Flying Laboratory, still in the company's house colours. BOEING

The US Air Force began studies for a replacement for the F-15 Eagle and F-16 Fighting Falcon in 1981. It planned to take advantage of new technology to create a fighter able to counter the new generation of Soviet combat aircraft and air defence systems under development. Known as the Advanced Tactical Fighter (ATF), the programme placed emphasis on low observability and the ability to supercruise - flying supersonically without having to resort to the use of an afterburner. Advanced integrated sensors were to be incorporated to give the pilot unprecedented situational awareness of the battlespace, so that the new fighter could detect and attack targets before they became aware of the threat – a capability encapsulated by the phrase 'first-look, first shot, first kill'. Stealth required that the platform radiated as few detectable electronic emissions as possible, but combining the requirement to remain undetected while finding its adversaries became one of the major challenges facing companies that studied proposals for ATF. The avionics and software development programme to 'square the circle' of the competing requirements of stealth and situational awareness would be large and complex. A flying testbed was required in order to test

An artist's impression of the internal configuration of the Boeing 757 Avionics Flying Laboratory.
BOEING

concepts and systems in the air, before the ATF prototypes were available.

Avionics Flying Laboratory

Although Boeing had submitted its own design proposal for ATF at the start of the Dem/Val (demonstration/validation) phase, in July 1986 it agreed with Lockheed and General Dynamics to co-operate on whichever of their designs was selected to go forward. Lockheed's design emerged as one of the two frontrunners in the US Air Force evaluation, while General Dynamics came third and Boeing fourth. Northrop Grumman and McDonnell Douglas formed a rival team. Both groups were awarded contracts for a pair of demonstrators, which were designated the YF-22 and YF-23, respectively.

Boeing's role in its group included integration of the avionics. It was hoped to be able to cut F-22 flight test hours by up to 50% by using a surrogate platform to test the sensors and software. The prototype Boeing 757-200 (N757A, c/n 22212) was available and was selected for modification as the Avionics Flying Laboratory (AFL). A pod was mounted under the nose, various protrusions sprouted under »

the rear fuselage and sensors fitted on the starboard wingtip. Workstations were installed in the cabin for more than 25 technicians, while most of the windows along the fuselage were blanked over. Flight tests with the AFL began on July 17, 1987, before the configuration of the fighter was frozen. AFL contributed more than 200 flight hours to the programme.

Modifications

The first of the YF-22s flew on September 29, 1990, and the Lockheed-led team was announced as the preferred ATF option on April 23, 1991. After securing a development contract for the F-22, the AFL was ferried to Boeing's facility at Wichita, Kansas, for more extensive modifications. The most prominent external change was the grafting of a F-22 nose section onto the forward pressure bulkhead of the airliner, adding about 9ft (2.74m) to its length. This would initially contain a developmental model of the Westinghouse/Texas Instruments (later Northrop Grumman/Raytheon) APG-77 solid-state, active electronically scanned array (AESA) radar, along with an inertial reference system, missile launch detector, a data link and microwave landing system. It was the radically altered nose profile that gave rise to the aircraft's Catfish nickname, although it was more formally known as the F-22 Flying Test Bed (FTB). A fully functional, representative F-22 cockpit was installed inside the cabin.

The FTB retuned to Boeing Field in Seattle, Washington, during June 1997. The APG-77 first flew on the aircraft on November 21, 1997. Between August and December 1998, a 26ft (7.92m) span wing, with a similar sweepback to that of the F-22, was mounted just behind the cockpit on the upper fuselage. Known as the sensor wing, it housed the ALR-94 electronic warfare, communication, navigation and identification (CNI) and other systems destined for the fighter. The information generated by the sensors was fed into a common integrated processor (CIP) that fused the data into a coherent whole for display in the cockpit. The sensor wing allowed the FTB to fully emulate the capabilities of the F-22 while running them on prototype software, allowing test engineers to monitor performance and utility.

Upgrading the Raptor

The FTB flew again following fitting out on March 11, 1999, initially running Block 1 software within the basic core operating system and radar. One of its first missions was to deploy to

The Boeing 757 was modified with the nose section of the F-22 which contained developmental versions of the APG-77 AESA radar.

Andrews Air Force Base, Maryland, to demonstrate the radar to the US Congress, which was concerned about the slow pace of development of the fighter's systems. While there, the FTB flew several missions, using F-16s assigned to the District of Columbia Air National Guard unit as radar targets, to highlight the performance of the AESA.

All software for the F-22 was originally flight tested on the aircraft. By late 1999, when Block 2 software was being run, the FTB had accumulated 360 hours of F-22 avionics testing. Block 3.0, the first combat-capable release, which included multi-sensor fusion, was flown in the aircraft from September 2000.

Development of F-22 software was a complicated process, involving over 1.7 million lines of code, and suffered several setbacks and delays. The years 2002 and 2003 saw the F-22 plagued by software instability issues. »

The radical alterations to the nose section of the Boeing 757 gave rise to its Catfish nickname.

Flying four to six hour sorties the FTB allowed flight critical software to be tested safely, as well as freeing up the limited F-22 trials fleet for other tasks. The instability problems were largely resolved by late 2004 and a year later the aircraft supported a redesign of the CNI, which involved separating it from the CIP to improve performance. In mid-2006, after this was completed, the Boeing 757 was placed into flyable storage at Seattle, where it was to remain for two years.

The FTB was revived again to support development of Increment 3.1 for the F-22, designed to improve the fighter's air-to-ground capabilities. From December 2007 the Boeing 757's cabin was refitted with new flat-panel displays at 30 workstations, while an APG-77(V)1 radar was installed in the nose with additional functionality, including a synthetic-aperture ground imaging mode and electronic attack capability, both core enhancements of the 3.1 upgrade. FTB returned to the air in June 2008.

The addition of the sensor wing above the cockpit allowed the Boeing 757 F-22 FTB to evaluate software used to control and add functionality to the conformal sensors embedded in the structure.

A ground-based adjunct to the flying testbed, known as the Agile Integration Laboratory (AIL), was developed to make the most of the FTB's capabilities. AIL was a trailer that accommodated additional hardware, instrumentation, and test equipment to perform system-level integration and development testing of the F-22 mission systems, to help fast track development of the new radar capabilities. AIL would be parked next to the aircraft and linked to it via an umbilical cord, allowing flight test data to be shared and evaluated alongside the operators in the 757's cabin.

Increment 3.1 was followed by Increment 3.2, a two-phase upgrade to enhance the fighter's capabilities in the air-to-air role. The Increment 3.2A phase focused on upgrades to electronic warfare, communications and identification systems. Update 6 incorporated cryptographic and avionics stability enhancements.

Although the FTB was frequently deployed away from Seattle, usually to Edwards Air Force Base, California, or other sites involved in F-22 testing, a major change in operations came on May 5, 2017, when the aircraft moved its base of operations to St Louis, Missouri. By then, it was also involved in the testing of prototype Increment 3.2B software, which introduced better geolocation capabilities and compatibility with the AIM-9X Sidewinder and AIM-120D AMRAAM air-to-air missiles. Implementation of the upgrade in the F-22 fleet began in 2019.

The FTB continues to play its role supporting the F-22 force and is likely to do so for some time to come, following the award of the Advanced Raptor Enhancement and Sustainment (ARES) contract to Lockheed Martin in November 2021. ARES includes provision for continuing upgrades, enhancements and fixes to the F-22's avionics and software and will run until October 2031, if all options are exercised. By then, Boeing 757 N757A will be four months shy of the 50th anniversary of its first flight.

A cutaway of the forward cabin of the F-22 FTB, showing the representative F-22 cockpit and workstations installed in the aircraft.

757 X-Planes

David Willis reviews the Boeing 757s that have found a second career as a testbed after being retired by the airlines.

O nly a handful of the 1,050 Boeing 757s built have been used as testbeds. The most prominent were the first and second aircraft built, which went on to become testbeds for the F-22 programme with Boeing and the Airborne Research Integrated Experiments System with NASA, both are detailed in separate articles in this volume. In addition, former airline Boeing 757s have been used by Honeywell, L-3 Communications, and Boeing as test platforms for various systems and technologies, while another aircraft is in the process of being modified to serve as demonstrator for the UK's latest combat aircraft project.

Honeywell's Testbed

Former MyTravel Boeing 757-225 G-JALC (c/n 22194) was acquired by Honeywell Aerospace in April 2005 after it had been retired by the airline to Lasham, Hampshire. It was registered to its new owner as N757HW and was ferried to Pinal Air Park, Arizona in October 2005 for repainting in Honeywell's colours. The company acquired the aircraft to serve as a testbed for both its powerplants and avionics.

Fifth off the production line at Renton, Washington, the airliner was originally built for Eastern Air Lines and served with that carrier as N504EA from February 1983 until going to the British scheduled and charter operator Airtours International Airways in early 1995. The airline changed its name in 2002 to MyTravel after a group rebranding exercise.

Honeywell added a stub wing on the starboard forward fuselage, with an aerodynamic fairing at the interface between the two structures, on which power plants could be mounted for inflight evaluation. Monitoring equipment and workstations were　>>

Honeywell's Boeing 757 has a pylon on the forward starboard side of the fuselage from which powerplants can be mounted for testing.
HONEYWELL

In addition to acting as a powerplant testbed, Honeywell's Boeing 757 has been used as a trials platform for avionics and inflight communication systems. HONEYWELL

CRAFT.
THE FUTURE IS WHAT WE MAKE IT.
Honeywell
#FUTURESHAPER

installed in the cabin so that the parameters of the test subjects could be observed and recorded. The aircraft was configured with 25 seats in the cabin, although during a typical test sortie it has a crew of seven, including the two pilots.

The company based its Boeing 757 at Phoenix Sky Harbor International Airport in Arizona, from where it made its first flight with three engines on December 20, 2008. The aircraft subsequently played a significant role in the testing of the HTF7000 turbofan engine series, as well as the TFE731 geared turbofan and TPE331 turboprop.

In addition to serving as an engine testbed, the aircraft was configured to evaluate and demonstrate avionics and communication systems, for which a blister was mounted on the upper rear of the fuselage to house the antennas required. Next generation flight management systems, 3D weather radars (including the IntuVue RDR-4000 and IntuVue RDR-7000), airborne Wi-Fi (such as Honeywell's JetWave and JetWave MCX) and satellite communications have all been tested on the platform. To highlight the role played developing inflight communication, the aircraft carried 'Connected Aircraft' titles along the top of the fuselage until 2021, when they were changed to 'The Future is What We Make It'.

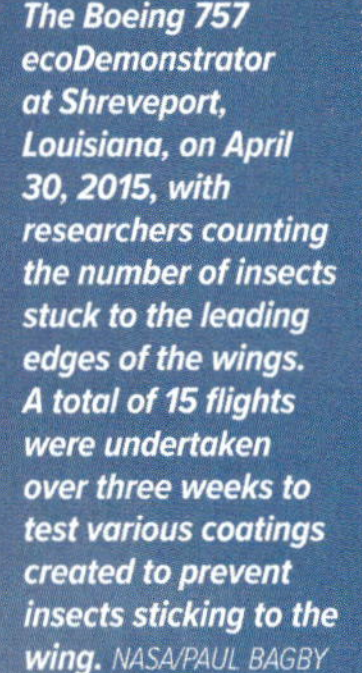

The Boeing 757 ecoDemonstrator at Shreveport, Louisiana, on April 30, 2015, with researchers counting the number of insects stuck to the leading edges of the wings. A total of 15 flights were undertaken over three weeks to test various coatings created to prevent insects sticking to the wing. NASA/PAUL BAGBY

The Boeing 757 is the largest aircraft in Honeywell's small test fleet. The company plans to continue to operate the former airliner for the foreseeable future. As of mid-2022 it had accumulated more than 3,000 hours during 800 flights with Honeywell, during which it has visited more than 30 countries.

Trailblazer

While Honeywell's use of the Boeing 757 has been well documented – and the aircraft has been displayed at several air shows – little information has emerged about the use of the type by L-3 Communications (later L3 Technologies and currently L3Harris Technologies).

Boeing 757-2Q8 OH-LBO (c/n 28172) was delivered to Finnair in October 1997 and served with the Finnish flag-carrier until September 2013. In November 2013 it was re-registered N903TB with L-3 Communications based at Majors Field in Greenville, Texas, from where it was reportedly used as an avionics testbed. Named *Trailblazer*, the aircraft had two large antenna blisters mounted on top of its fuselage and a Texan star on its fin. Its civil registration was cancelled in July 2018 and the aircraft was delivered to the US Air Force as C-32A 19-0018, joining the Special Air Mission fleet of the 89th

Airlift Wing at Joint Base Andrews, Maryland.

Various other Boeing 757s have been associated with different divisions of L-3 over the years, although exactly what they have been used for has not been disclosed. In August and November 2018 757-26D N473AP (c/n 24473) and 757-260 N752LT (c/n 26058) were acquired from Lance Toland Ltd and registered to L-3 Communications Advanced Aviation of Helena, Montana. The former was noted landing at Long Beach Daugherty Field, California, in December 2019 in its former OpenSkies scheme minus titles, while the latter is reportedly stored at Majors Field. The former NASA Boeing 757-225, N144DC (c/n 22191), which was acquired in April 2009, also remains registered to L-3 Capital.

ecoDemonstrator

Boeing was the first to make use of the 757 as a testbed, modifying the first aircraft built to test and validate the avionics and systems for the Lockheed Martin F-22 Raptor. It was not the only example of the airliner used by the manufacturer as a testbed, however, as a 757 was selected as the third aircraft for Boeing's ecoDemonstrator programme, which has the broad aim of investigating technology that may be of environmental benefit. These include methods of improving fuel efficiency, reducing noise, and decreasing the footprint of airliner operations. Since it was launched in 2010, nine individual aircraft of five basic types have been used in the programme, including a 757-200.

The project was undertaken in collaboration with NASA, under its Environmentally Responsible Aviation programme, and the TUI Group, in which colours the aircraft (N757ET c/n 24627) was painted. It had spent its passenger-carrying career with United Airlines, flying with the American carrier as N506UA for 23 years.

The aircraft was modified to investigate the utility of natural laminar and active flow control technology on future airliners, using active flow control over the vertical tail and new wing leading-edge sections. Experimental coatings, designed to stop dead insects accreting on surfaces, were added to eight panels on the second and third leading-edge slats of the starboard wing, while a variable camber Krüger flap on a 22ft (6.7m) glove section was added to the port wing. The section was deployed when the airliner transited altitudes where insects are prevalent, protecting the leading-edge from biological matter than can disrupt natural laminar flow over the wing. It retracted into the lower wing section when not required.

As part of the active flow control tests the 757 had both a Pratt & Whitney PW2037 and a PW2040 engine fitted, the latter's additional thrust allowing greater asymmetric forces to be applied. This was to be countered by 31 active flow control actuator exit nozzles or sweeping jet actuators added on the starboard side of the tail, which were designed to increase rudder effectiveness. Mounted just behind the rudder's leading edge, the nozzles provided cooled, pressurised air fed from the auxiliary power unit, which helped the airflow remain attached to the surface of the tail. The nozzles increased the authority of the rudder, which could result in smaller tails for future airliners, with a corresponding reduction in airframe weight and drag, and thus lower fuel burn.

Post modification, the airliner first flew from Boeing Field in Seattle, Washington, on March 17, 2015. Much of the test flying was undertaken near Shreveport, Louisiana, at altitudes below 10,000ft (3,048m) where insect life was abundant, the multiple deaths being recorded by cameras covering the accretion insect mitigation panels. The active flow control system was evaluated over the Strait of Juan de Fuca near Seattle. When it was activated, the pilots reported the 757 flew smoother and rudder control authority was increased.

The 757 ecoDemonstrator was withdrawn from use on July 7, but the end of the flight test programme was not the end of the aircraft's contribution to 'green' research. Under an agreement reached with the Aircraft Fleet Recycling Association, the airliner was broken up using new methods with the aim of reducing the amount of residual material »

Although painted in TUI colours, the Boeing 757 ecoDemonstrator never actually served with the airline. The dots on the tail are devices to help visualise the flow of air over the surface created by the active flow control system.
BOEING/JOHN D PARKER

Seen in a photograph released in December 2024, the Excalibur Flight Test Aircraft reveals new side and belly pods.
DAVE TURNBULL - QINETIQ

and releasing fewer hazardous chemicals into the environment. It was dismantled at Grant County International Airport at Moses Field, Washington, in September 2015.

Boeing 757-204 G-BYAW, at Lasham in September 2022, is reported to be the airframe being modified as Excalibur.
DAVID WILLIS

Excalibur

The latest Boeing 757 destined to be modified as a testbed is Excalibur, a trials platform for systems under consideration for the UK-led Tempest sixth-generation Tempest Future Combat Air System. Excalibur is due to prove technology in the air to lower risk in the Tempest programme, including communications, radar and other sensors, under the digital first approach adopted for the aircraft's electronics. A representative virtual cockpit is planned for installation in the cabin.

In addition to supporting Tempest, it is envisaged that Excalibur will be made available to international partners and the wider industry, as well as support capability enhancements for the RAF's Eurofighter Typhoon and Lockheed Martin F-35B Lightning fleets.

Plans for Excalibur were first revealed in July 2019. Responsibility for the project is vested with 2Excel

Another late 2024 image of Excalibur displaying the new side and belly pods..
DAVE TURNBULL - QINETIQ

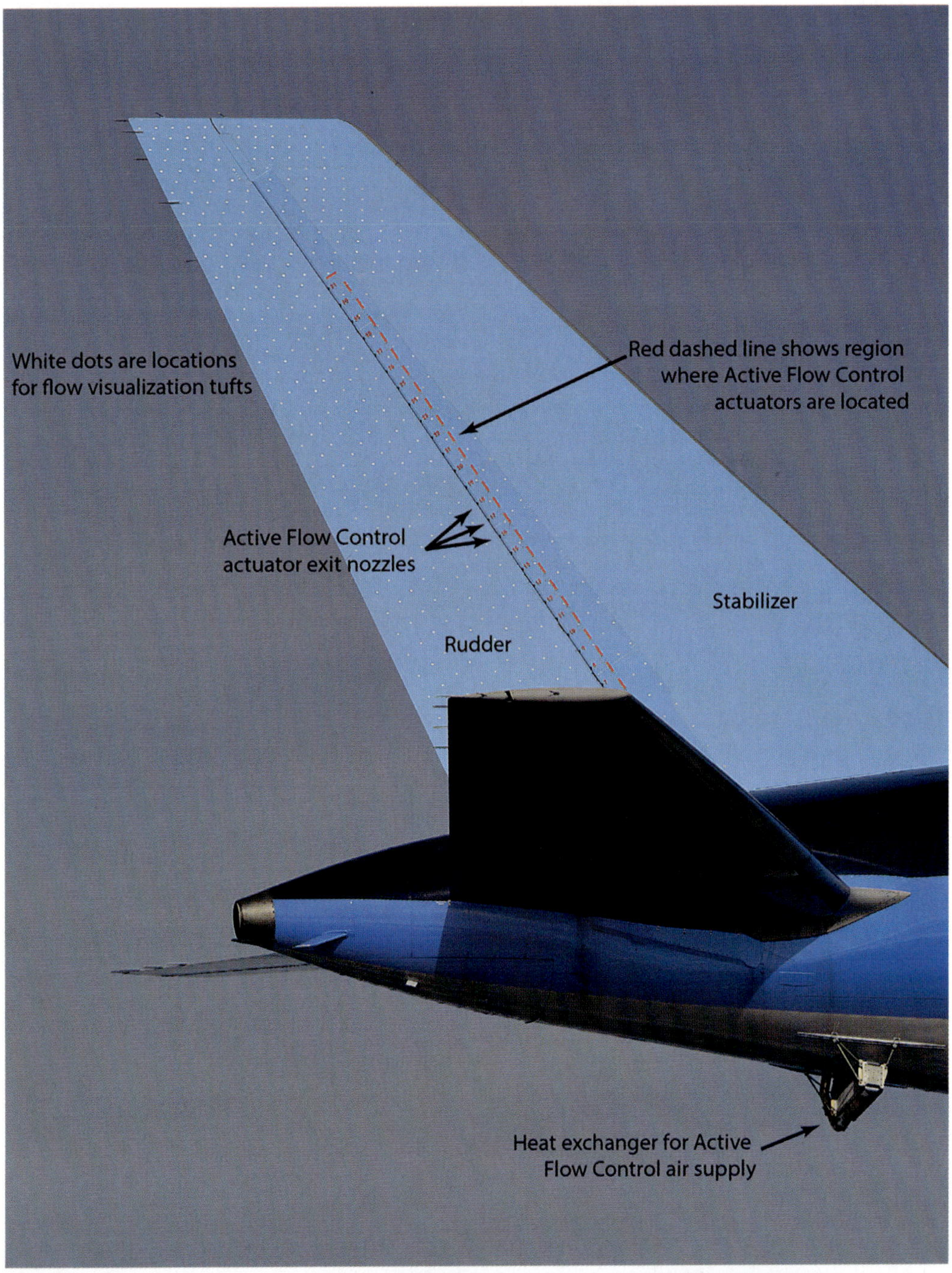

NASA's green aviation tests included the Active Flow Control Enhanced Vertical Tail Flight Experiment, for which 31 tiny devices called sweeping jet actuators were installed on the tail of a Boeing 757 ecoDemonstrator aircraft to determine what – if any – impact the devices had on the aerodynamics of the tail. NASA/BOEING

which the size, weight and power requirements of the technology planned to fly on Excalibur was considered. Criteria such as power, cooling, racking, observer stations, computing and data recording facilities were investigated, while external and internal modifications were modelled. It was announced in September 2021 that Phase 2 had begun, during which the companies will survey, inspect, and confirm the proposed installation solutions. At the time, the phase was expected to last 12 months.

In December 2024, Leonardo announced that Excalibur had successfully completed its first phase of modification and flight testing. The milestone saw Excalibur assessed for stability during flight. The aircraft was then due for further engineering work at QinetiQ's Boscombe Down facility in Wiltshire.

The first phase of modification saw the Excalibur FTA equipped with new side and belly pods, changing the outer mould line of the aircraft. These pods are designed to host the Integrated Sensors, Non-Kinetic Effects (ISANKE) and Integrated Communications Systems (ICS) that Leonardo and its international partners are developing as part of their work on GCAP. Further modification to the Excalibur FTA aircraft will include a fighter jet-style nose cone, to host advanced radar-based sensor demonstrators.

The focus of the Excalibur programme will soon move to the installation of ISANKE & ICS demonstrator systems on-board, which will allow scientists and engineers aboard to test and refine the systems whilst in flight.

Aviation, a British aviation services business, under contract from Team Tempest partner Leonardo. The 757 was selected as a testbed in preference to a Boeing 737 because of its larger cabin and performance, while each of its Rolls-Royce RB211-535 (plus the auxiliary power unit) can generate up to 90kVA of electrical power, vital for the systems to be evaluated. The larger design is also capable of carrying 14,500kg (31,967lb) of payload with a full fuel load and the 2.5m (8ft 2in) of clearance between the fuselage and ground allows bulky equipment to be carried under the aircraft.

What is understood to be Excalibur's airframe, former TUI Boeing 757-204 G-BYAW (c/n 27234) built in 1995, arrived at 2Excel's large aircraft engineering facility at Lasham, Hampshire on November 11, 2019, after being withdrawn from service by TUI Airways a week earlier. The airliner was delivered new to Britannia Airways in April 1995 and remained with the charter carrier when it was rebranded as Thomsonfly in May 2005 and Thomson Airways in November 2008 (after merging with First Choice Airways), before becoming TUI in October 2017.

2Excel's in-house design office has already completed a two-year Phase 1 feasibility study for the project, during

To the Four
Winds

For 20 years the Royal New Zealand Air Force has operated two Boeing 757s. The aircraft have performed many and varied missions from Antarctica to the Pacific Islands, and from the Middle East to Europe, but a replacement is overdue. **Jim Winchester** reports.

Boeing 757-2K2 *NZ7571 during a flight demonstration at RAF Fairford during a RIAT display.* AIRTEAMIMAGES/ PHILLIPPE NORET

The Royal New Zealand Air Force (RNZAF) disbanded its air combat force at the end of 2001, leaving two Boeing 727-200s as its only jet aircraft in service with No.40 Squadron. The former United Airlines aircraft (serial numbers NZ7271 and NZ7272) entered RNZAF service in 1981, joining the unit's five Lockheed C-130H Hercules based at Whenuapai in greater Auckland.

The demise of the A-4K Skyhawk and Aermacchi MB.339 jet squadrons, which came about for political rather than budgetary reasons, was unpopular within the RNZAF but did free up money for other things. The government's Long Term Development Plan (LTDP) for defence issued in June 2002 called for NZD$1bn to be spent on upgrading and renewing essential elements of the air force. By this time its Boeing 727s were showing signs of corrosion and were facing increasing noise restrictions at airports worldwide.

Replacement of the 727s was becoming a priority and a Fixed Wing Transport Review was begun in July 2002. In November a report was issued recommending a life-extension of the C-130s, which had been purchased in 1965-1969, and replacement of the 727s with two second-hand Boeing 757s, modified for strategic transport tasks.

From Transavia

After 9/11 with the slump in commercial airline traffic, bargains on used airliners could be had and the government purchased two 757-2K2s from Dutch airline Transavia, which operated eight 2K2s with RB211-535 E4 engines between 1992 and 2004. The 757 had never been operated by any New Zealand airline, but neither had the 727. They would be the largest aircraft in RNZAF history.

The two 757s chosen were built alongside each other at Boeing's Renton plant. PH-TKA (c/n 26633) made its first flight on January 22, 1993 and was delivered to Transavia Airlines a month later. After a decade of service on the Dutch operator's holiday routes, it made its last flight between Palma and Amsterdam on March 16, 2003. PH-TKB (c/n 26634) had a very similar history: first flight April 15, 1993; delivery to Transavia on May 3, 1993; last service Rhodes-Amsterdam on March 16, 2003.

Both were sold by Transavia to GECAS before being sold on to the RNZAF and were flown to Bristol Filton for repainting in RNZAF colours, then to Shannon for maintenance, before setting off on their delivery flights » to New Zealand. NZ7571 (the former PH-TKA) arrived on May 7 and NZ7572 (the former PH-TKB) on June 30, 2003.

The 1968-built 727s were put into storage in April and May 2003, although NZ7271 was briefly reactivated in June to cover delays to the delivery of the second 757. It was exported to Swaziland as 3D-KMJ in November 2004. NZ7272 was used as a break room by the Technical Training School at RNZAF Woodbourne before being dismantled in 2019, with large parts going to the RNZAF Museum at Wigram. Each Boeing 727 had more than 46,000 hours on the clock by the time they were retired.

The two 757s were declared operational in the passenger role by July 2003, but the plan was always to convert them to a multi-role, flexible standard. Cost of the project including acquisition and modification was given as NZD$221m, with the purchase price of NZD$108.2m and NZD$112.4m for the conversion to combi passenger-freight configuration and other upgrades.

Initially the 757s retained their standard seating arrangement while negotiations continued with potential contractors for the modification work. The hold freight compartments could be used for more than baggage. A 757 delivered 24 Javelin missiles and simulators from the United States to Auckland

and regular flights carrying troops on exercise and deployment. In 2006 the 757s transported police and soldiers after riots in Honiara, the Solomon Islands and Nuku'alofa, Tonga, helping the local police to re-establish order.

An unusual mission that year was participation in Pacific Protector 2006, a Proliferation Security Initiative (PSI) exercise held in Australia. In one scenario a 757 acted as an interception target for RAAF F/A-18 Hornets, playing an airliner suspected of carrying illicit cargo.

Multirole Conversion

In November 2005, Singapore Technologies Aerospace was selected as prime contractor with the work to be performed by its subsidiary Mobile Aerospace Engineering in Mobile, Alabama with specialist design and support from Boeing Commercial and Boeing Integrated Defense Systems. NZ7571 was inducted to MAE in Mobile on April 16, 2007 for passenger to freighter conversion and an avionics upgrade and other work to enhance the capability of the aircraft in remote operating environments. This included fitting a large freight door on the forward port fuselage, adding a strengthened floor, a new cargo handling system, integral air stairs for the rear passenger door, and a crew boarding

ladder in the nose wheel bay. Engine thrust was increased and new civil and military communications systems were fitted.

The test programme began on June 22, 2008 with a four-hour flight from Mobile's Brookley Field. After four more sorties to measure cabin noise and test the military navigation and communication systems, the programme was completed on July 23 and the 757 welcomed home at Wellington on August 20. The second aircraft arrived at RNZAF Ohakea on February 12, 2009.

Antarctic Ops

Since 1965, the RNZAF has supported scientific efforts in Antarctica, sharing its aircraft and resources in a joint United States – New Zealand logistics pool. Initially the RNZAF contribution was use of a C-130H because the Boeing 727 was not cleared to land on the ice runway at Pegasus Field, McMurdo Sound, mainly because it lacked the range.

After the operational test and evaluation (OT&E) period a 757 made the first trial Antarctic flights on December 16, 2009 and February 11, 2010. Before the inaugural flight a thorough inspection of the engine filters was conducted by the New Zealand Defence Technology Agency. Excessive particles were found in one

NZ7571 displaying at RAF Cosford.
AIRTEAMIMAGES/STUART LAWSON

filter, indicating imminent bearing failure and the initial intention was for the engine to be changed. However, at the cost of a NZD$300,000 bearing repair, an expensive engine replacement at around ten times as much was avoided. As was a potentially dangerous and certainly challenging situation if complete failure had occurred en route to or in Antarctica.

Following the successful completion of these missions, the 757 was included in the logistics pool, used primarily over the subsequent three years for returning personnel at the end of the summer season. For 2013-2014, the 757 was used to deliver people at the start of the season. Since then the frequency has increased, with six 757 flights scheduled between September 2021 and March 2022, alongside nine C-130 supply missions.

On October 7, 2013 NZ7571 made a landing below weather minima at Pegasus Field. A loaded 757 cannot carry the fuel needed to make a flight from Christchurch to McMurdo and return without landing. At the point of safe return, three hours into the four-and-a-half-hour flight, when the decision had to be made to proceed or return to Christchurch, the crew was assured weather at the airfield would be within the landing criteria at the expected arrival time, but 20 minutes later thick fog rolled in. The 757 circled overhead for two hours then made two missed approaches. On the third, the runway lights were spotted at an altitude of approximately 110ft (34m) and the aircraft made a safe landing with 13 crew and 117 passengers including a senior government minister. A subsequent enquiry praised the pilots' actions but noted that the potential consequences of the weather deteriorating were elevated for the Boeing 757 aircraft because of the lack of alternative approach procedures and aerodromes suitable for the aircraft type.

Operations and Demonstrations

The RNZAF's 757s provided strategic airlift in support of the Provincial Reconstruction Team (PRT) operating in Afghanistan's Bamiyan Province, flying personnel and supplies into the UAE for onward movement into theatre by C-130H. On one occasion a 757 delivered crew and spare parts, including a propeller, to the Middle East to fix a P-3K2 Orion assigned to 5 Squadron which was supporting Combined Task Force 150 on counter-terrorism and anti-smuggling operations over the Arabian Sea.

Humanitarian assistance and disaster relief (HADR) is another mission the 757 has been tasked to do on numerous occasions. After the 2011 Christchurch earthquake, 40 Squadron's 757s and Hercules ran continuous return flights in a 24-hour operation bringing in supplies and evacuating people from the city to Wellington and Auckland. This was the single biggest movement of personnel and freight ever carried out by the RNZAF.

Cyclone Winston in February 2016 caused severe destruction in Fiji. RNZAF P-3K2 Orion maritime patrol aircraft made initial reconnaissance flights and a C-130 dropped urgent supplies 24 hours after the storm's passage. Delivered by 757, an inter-agency joint reconnaissance team was on the ground in the capital Suva within 72 hours of the cyclone, to work with the local government to assess the damage and plan the response, particularly for key government infrastructure such as health facilities, drinking water, and schools.

The New Zealand Defence Force carries out regular exercises with the nation's Pacific neighbours, such as Tropic Astra, which gives experience in operating in tropical conditions. »

The 2009 edition saw over 100 RNZAF personnel and 90 army officer cadets transported to Samoa for a month-long exercise.

Political unrest in the Solomon Islands has seen New Zealand troops and police deploy under Operation Solomons Assist. Personnel were initially deployed in December 2021 in a 757 followed by airlift of vehicles in a C-130.

At the start of COVID-19-related travel restrictions in 2020, 757s returned 119 New Zealanders stranded in Vanuatu and took 1,000 Vanuatuan seasonal workers home. The 757s delivered personal protective equipment and medical teams to Papua New Guinea in March and November 2021 following spikes in COVID-19 cases there. After a measles outbreak in Samoa, a 757 airlifted nearly three tonnes of vaccines, refrigerators and other medical supplies.

In the aeromedical evacuation (AME) role, the 757s can be equipped with a roll-on, roll-off system of pallets for transport of medium dependency and/or high dependency patients, and medical workstation units.

The 757 can move a company-sized group of around 140 soldiers in all-economy class seating. In 2012, a 757 took New Zealand Army engineers to an exercise in California and returned 104 US Marines to New Zealand for the commemoration of the 70th anniversary of the 1st Marine Division being stationed in New Zealand during World War Two.

The Boeings are semi-regular visitors to the UK, performing various logistics taskings. One mission is transporting participants in the Long Look exchange programme. Since 1976, New Zealand and British personnel have swapped places to experience how each other operates. In recent times this has involved a core of 25 British Army soldiers or Royal Marines travelling to New Zealand for four months, and 25 New Zealand Army personnel travelling to the UK to work and train with British forces. The Royal Air Force and Royal Navy also participates in these exchanges. A 757 isn't always used for such relatively small groups of personnel, but taskings can be combined with freight movements. In mid-2009 a 757 was sent to Italy to collect the part-task trainer for the RNZAF's new AgustaWestland (now Leonardo) AW109 light utility helicopters.

The RNZAF 757 is one of the largest military aircraft to routinely perform air display routines. No. 40 Squadron has performed display routines in New Zealand, Australia and the United Kingdom.

The six-minute display routine begins with a low pass flown into wind at 350kts and 100ft (30.5m) followed by a 2g pull up to between 45o and 55 o nose up pitch into a zoom climb ending at an altitude between 8,000 and 10,000ft (2,438-3,050m) depending on the type of pull up used. The sequence ends with a 60° wingover at around 220kts.

NZ7572 makes a pass at RAF Waddington. AIRTEAMIMAGES/CHRIS PROCTOR

RNZAF Boeing 757s wear a black triple cheatline along the fuselage and around the nose. DAVID EVANS

RNZAF crew push palletised cargo on the strengthened floor of a Boeing 757-2K2. *ROYAL NEW ZEALAND AIR FORCE*

VIP Role

One mis-perception of the 757's role is that the aircraft are primarily used for transporting politicians on overseas trips, but this role is performed less regularly than personnel and freight hauling. The most common VIP use is to transport a prime ministerial delegation to trade talks or international conferences. The capacity of the Boeing allows not only the PM and staff from the Department of the Prime Minister and Cabinet to travel, but also officials from the Ministry of Foreign Affairs and Trade (MFAT) and the New Zealand Trade and Enterprise (NZTE) agency and invited industry guests, members of the parliamentary press gallery and Diplomatic Protection Squad security personnel. For the VIP role a booth is situated in the forward cabin, containing a teleprinter and other secure communications equipment.

The VIP seating is far from luxurious. The first-class section more closely resembles a business class cabin from the 1990s. A separate section includes chairs and tables in club layout for work purposes though the cabin is mostly configured in economy style. There is no in-flight entertainment system, but good quality food is served by RNZAF flight stewards.

RNZAF crew prepare to lift palletised cargo for loading onboard a 757 via the main cargo door. ROYAL NEW ZEALAND AIR FORCE

»

Another use is by Veterans' Affairs NZ to attend overseas commemorations, such as anniversaries of the Gallipoli campaign, VE and VJ Day. Seats for these are usually allocated on a ballot basis and are flown at full capacity.

Decreasing Reliability

Unlike a 757 in regular airline service, which essentially flies all day every day between periods of scheduled maintenance, the RNZAF's aircraft fly comparatively infrequently, with a change in cabin configuration often taking place between missions. No.40 Squadron is allocated around 1,450 757 flight hours per year, a mix of long and short sectors, operational and training flights at a wide range of weights. By comparison a 757 in regular airline service might fly nearly 3,000 hours annually, most of them similar distances and loads.

As a result of this style of operation and increasing age, the RNZAF 757's reliability has declined, leading to some embarrassing situations on VIP missions in particular. On a trade trip to India in 2016, a 757 made two aborted take-off attempts at Townsville, Australia and a second aircraft had to be sent to rescue then-Prime Minister John Key and a delegation of

The appearance of RNZAF 757s has changed little in two decades. The gloss grey paint is Federal Standard Colour (FS16251), the same shade applied to RNZAF P-3K2s. ROYAL NEW ZEALAND AIR FORCE

nearly 100. In 2019 Prime Minister Jacinda Ardern suffered a week of 757 breakdowns and the deputy PM was stranded in Vanuatu in a separate incident. The second 757 was dispatched to bring him back. A local news organisation obtained documents that showed the Boeing 757 fleet was unavailable for a total of 156 days between the beginning of 2019 and May 2021. During the Taliban takeover of Afghanistan in 2021 a C-130H was sent to evacuate New Zealand citizens and local staff from Kabul. The government stated that a Hercules was the only feasible option for this deployment due to the low availability of the ageing Boeing 757 fleet.

Between October 2017 and June 2022, more than NZD $70m was spent on unplanned maintenance and 1,561 mechanical faults recorded, with six safety incidents occurring that required the aircraft to divert or abort their task. Engine overhauls that once took 90 days were taking 300 days and two extra engines had to be bought to make sure the aircraft could be available.

Boeings Going

Given the C-130Hs and P-3K2s have marked their 50th birthdays in RNZAF service, in August 2016 the government issued a request for information for aircraft to ensure continued air mobility and air surveillance operations beyond 2020. At the time the aim was to have the first Hercules replacement delivered

A Boeing 757-2K2 on the ice runway at Pegasus Field, McMurdo Sound Antarctica. Since 1965, the RNZAF has supported scientific efforts in Antarctica, sharing its aircraft and resources in a joint United States – New Zealand logistics pool. ROYAL NEW ZEALAND AIR FORCE

The RNZAF 757s feature the compass marking of 40 Squadron on the fin and wear large full-colour national insignia and fin flash. ROYAL NEW ZEALAND AIR FORCE

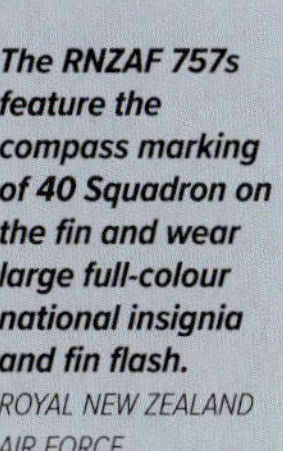

by February 2020 and the first B757-200 replacement to follow by February 2025. These requirements evolved and split into a Future Air Surveillance Capability – which was met by the selection of the Boeing P-8 Poseidon in July 2018 – and a Future Air Mobility Capability to provide both tactical and strategic airlift. The government came close to acquiring the last Boeing C-17s off the production line but would ideally have wanted more than just the two available. Other contenders, which could theoretically have provided a 'one size fits all' solution included the Kawasaki C-2 and Airbus A400M, but the selection of the Lockheed Martin C-130J Super Hercules in June 2020 left the 757-replacement question open for a FAMC Phase 2.

On December 19, 2024 the New Zealand Ministry of Defence made an official announcement regarding the 757s. It said: "Defence has released a tender to market for proposals to replace the Royal New Zealand Air Force's two Boeing 757s by the end of 2027. The cost of maintaining and issues with reliability of the current fleet, alongside the competitiveness of the market for aircraft of this type, has meant the business case process has been fast tracked.

"This procurement seeks to replace these aircraft with commercially available, off-the-shelf Boeing 737 MAX 8 or Airbus A321 narrow-body aircraft. The tender process is designed to select a preferred provider for the replacement of the B757 aircraft. The information provided will be used to inform the final business case for Cabinet consideration.".

C-32
and Beyond

David Isby profiles Boeing 757s in service with the US Air Force.

Painted in a stylish blue-and-white livery, a stars-and-stripes flag marking on the fin and 'United States of America' titling on the fuselage, all four C-32As are recognisable world-wide as VVIP (very, very important person) transport aircraft. Assigned to the 89th Airlift Wing based at Joint Base Andrews in Maryland and operated by the 1st Airlift Squadron, the four jets meet the requirements of the 89th's Special Air Mission Foreign team.

The C-32As often use the *Air Force Two* callsign when carrying the vice president, one of the VVIPs that, over the years, has made frequent use of the type.

The C-32A also functions as *Air Force One* when carrying the president if the destination airport is too small to accommodate a Boeing VC-25A – the usual type for the role: The C-32A is cleared to use 5,000-foot runways.

A C-32A usually accompanies the president during long-distance trips, serving as a back-up to *Air Force One*.

In addition to transporting the president, vice-president, and the speaker, C-32As also carry other congressional leaders or delegations, cabinet secretaries, the first lady and justices of the Supreme Court. They are also used by senior Department of Défense leaders.

C-32A

From its launch, the twin-engine Boeing 757 replaced many earlier single-aisle airliners, most notably the Boeing 707 series. In the late 1990s, the 757 was seen as a potential replacement for the US Air Force VC-137, a VVIP version of the 707. Boeing had marketed a military transport version of the 757 to the US Air Force, that offered increased fuel efficiency and decreased operating costs; 757s powered by Pratt & Whitney PW2000-series engines would have provided commonality with Boeing C-17 Globemaster transport aircraft.

A rapid response was made possible by legislation enabling the use of commercial, off-the-shelf acquisition practices, less than two years from contract award to aircraft delivery.

Four 757-200s were converted to C-32As

at Boeing's Wichita, Kansas facility. Ordered on August 8, 1996, the first C-32A, serial number 98-0001 (c/n 29025), was delivered on June 1, 1998. The second aircraft (98-0002 c/n 29026) arrived at Andrews three days later, the remaining two (99-0003 c/n 29027 and 99-0004 c/n 29028) in November and December.

According to the US Air Force, the C-32A is equipped with the traffic collision avoidance system - the enhanced ground proximity warning system that gives advance warning of possible air and ground threats; a predictive wind shear warning system; the future air navigation system with global positioning and flight management system/ electronic flight instrument system.

C-32A conversion included fitting communications systems that meet the presidential requirement for constant and redundant connectivity.

Range was increased to 5,000nm (9,260km) by fitting additional 1,850 US gal (7,000 lit) fuel tanks in the forward and aft cargo holds, along with a 100-gal (378 lit) fresh water »

C-32A 09-0016 on final approach to London-Heathrow. *AIRTEAMIMAGES/ENDA BURKE*

Showing the interior of a C-32A before the 2016 upgrade, with then Secretary of Defense Robert Gates and former president George Bush in October 2006. DOD/ CHERIE THURLBY

supply. A self-deploying forward airstair and crew ladder were also installed.

Aft of the flight deck, the forward section of the fuselage includes a communication centre, a galley, lavatory and ten business-class seats.

Aft of that is the fully enclosed stateroom for the use of the primary passenger with its own changing area, lavatory, entertainment system, two first-class swivel seats and a convertible divan that seats three and folds out to a bed.

The third section contains the conference and staff facility with eight business class seats and the aftermost section has 32 business-class seats, a galley, two lavatories and closets for staff and accompanying media.

According to details available from the US Air Force, because the C-32 is a high-standing aircraft, it is easier to see under and around it – an important security factor for protecting the aircraft and its passengers.

From the original baseline configuration, C-32As have been incrementally upgraded, with aircraft designated for the *Air Force One* mission receiving priority.

In 2005, Boeing-developed and produced bulkheads to protect the cargo bay fuel tanks in the event of a hard landing.

At a total cost of $5m, in 2007, C-32As received Boeing-designed blended winglets, installed by Goodrich Aviation Technical Services in Everett Washington. These provide better efficiency on long-range flights.

Due to a potential for fuel vapour explosion in fuselage fuel tanks, the Federal Aviation Administration mandated the four C-32A aircraft had to undergo fuel tank flammability reduction modifications. US Air Force C-32As maintain Federal Aviation Administration (FAA) certification.

To meet the FAA mandate, by 2018, the C-32As received an improved nitrogen generation system (NGS), under a contract valued at $16.5m. The C-32 NGS modification was based on similar Boeing 757 installations but tailored to incorporate the auxiliary fuselage fuel tanks. The NGS supplies

nitrogen enriched air to all fuselage fuel tanks to reduce the risk of vapour explosion.

An interior upgrade contract, awarded in 2018 at a cost of $16.07m per aircraft, included refurbishing the VVIP/VIP sections to make them comparable with those on the VC-25As. New seating, furniture, carpets, and lighting lead to criticism of unnecessary luxury in the press. This upgrade included fitting triple-seat passenger accommodation to replace the previous business-class seats. A current modification programme is replacing seats in the forward section with four fully reclining crew rest seats, enabling missions longer than the current 16-hour limit without pre-positioning relief crews.

At least two refurbishment contracts were awarded to Boeing by the Air Force Life Cycle Management Center, Tinker Air Force Base, Oklahoma, one in 2017 and one the following year.

Official details of the 2017 contract valued at $18m released by the US Air Force stated the contract was for engineering support services for refurbishment of the interior for one of the C-32A aircraft. This included an FAA-approved upgrade to the C-32A interior, consisting of Group A kits for one aircraft First Article, and installation and testing along with the identification and procurement of long lead items for one aircraft. Work was due to be predominantly performed in Greenville, Texas, and was expected to be complete by August 31, 2018.

Official details of a 2018 contract awarded to Boeing released by the US Air Force stated the contract was for engineering support services for C-32 interior refresh second aircraft.

The C-32A interior requirements were for an appearance more commensurate with presidential section of the VC-25A. The requirements necessitated a combination of the following: upgraded interior elements; refurbished interior elements; painting and cleaning; replacing double-seat configuration with triple-seat configuration, aft of door three. Work was to be performed in Oklahoma City, Oklahoma; and various locations, and was expected to be completed by August 8, 2019.

Infrared countermeasures (IRCM) were first fitted to the C-32A aircraft in 2006. Previously, the jets were restricted from landing in Iraq due to their vulnerability to missile threats. Because some C-32As are used to carry the president into overseas airports, they were afforded the same level of protection against a range of threats as the larger VC-25As. On June 16, 2010, Northrop Grumman announced that its AAQ-24(V) Large Aircraft Infra-Red Counter Measures (LAIRCM) system equips head-of-state aircraft, which may indicate that the system is part of the C-32A IRCM upgrade, which would provide commonality with the IRCMs on other 89th AW twin-jet aircraft.

The communications system on board the C-32A is central to its mission set. Designed by the 645th Aeronautical Systems Group (dubbed the Big Safari programme office based at Wright-Patterson Air Force Base, Ohio) and implemented by a team led by L-3 Communications, it is the most significant recent upgrade; C-32As received multiple dorsal antennas and two satellite communications radomes.

Providing high-speed secure voice and internet connectivity while meeting the extremely demanding ≫

A C-32A parks at Joint Base Andrews, Maryland on December 17, 2014, carrying Alan Gross on his return from five-years of captivity in Cuba. US AIR FORCE/ MSGT KEVIN WALLACE

requirements for the Global Secure Information Management System (GSIMS) for highly classified content, the communication system appears compatible with the Multi-Role Tactical Common Data Link (MR-TCDL), which provides extremely fast exchange of data via Ka/Ku band satellite and line-of-sight connectivity.

Dorsal and ventral antennas connect with terrestrial relays.

Speaking at the time of a flight demonstration of the upgrades, Technical Sergeant Barry Bonnema the liaison between L3 and the 89th AW said: "These mods take several months to complete as the aircraft communication systems, including all the electrical harnesses, are completely upgraded, and brought up to state-of-the-art systems. While many new systems were installed, several of the legacy systems were maintained for redundancy and back-up purposes. These 89th AW aircraft have layer after layer of redundancy so if one system becomes inoperable, the Communication Systems Operator [CSO] can quickly switch to another system and restore the communications."

Staff Sergeant John Operana, a 1st Airlift Squadron CSO, said: "The comms system was upgraded from a proprietary fibre channel distribution system to an IP [internet protocol] based open architecture distribution system enabling centralised command and control capabilities. A Ka [frequency band]-based network was also added which increased bandwidth about 10-fold from previous system capability. Airborne executive phones [AEP] were also integrated to allow a single handset access to multiple classification voice connectivity."

The type of AEP, produced by L-3 Communications, is the same as used aboard VC-25As.

Funding for additional system upgrades was included in the FY2021 budget request and is planned to continue until FY2027. In FY2023, two C-32As will receive Senior Leader Communications to upgrade bandwidth, in-flight information, and commercial Wi-Fi, and installation of advanced voice and data user interface systems.

Four additional C-32As were acquired by the US Air Force between 2010 and 2019: 99-0015 (c/n 25044 in 2010), 99-0016 (c/n 28016 in 2011), 99-0017 (c/n 26272 in 2012) and 99-0018 (c/n 28172 in 2019). All four serve with the 89th Airlift Wing at Joint Base Andrews, Maryland, and were previously operated by commercial airlines.

C-32A Operations

The four C-32As are operated and maintained by the same aircrew and technicians responsible for *Air Force One*. Like *Air Force One*, the 89th AW's C-32As are operated and maintained to standards above and beyond those associated with other US Air Force aircraft. Components or systems are replaced at more frequent intervals and checked by more people than in other

C-32A 98-0002 takes off at Munich. *AIRTEAMIMAGES/ENA MONMORADO*

Marine Corps General Joseph Dunford, then chairman of the Joint Chiefs of Staff, works in his cabin aboard a C-32A on August 19, 2017. *DEPARTMENT OF DEFENSE/PETTY OFFICER 1ST CLASS DOMINIQUE PINEIRO*

units, reflected in a higher per-hour flight operating cost.

Personnel of the Presidential Airlift Group, 89th Operations Group and 89th Maintenance Group are selectively hired into their positions. This has made them an elite force.

The 89th AW flies hundreds of special air missions each year, which use the SAM radio callsign.

Speaking in 2016, the then-89th AW commander Colonel John Millard said: "It takes a dedicated airman to serve the president, vice president and our other distinguished customers. We flew more than 200 SAM missions to 75 countries in 2015 alone and did so with zero mishaps and a 98.4% departure reliability rate."

When a VVIP flies on a C-32A, often with members of the media onboard, any delay or problem with the aircraft will receive press coverage. Over the course of 2014, then-Secretary of State John Kerry had four C-32As break down while he was travelling. Twice, he, his staff and accompanying journalists had to return to Washington by commercial airline. In 2018, a flight with the first lady and a cabinet secretary on board had to be aborted after smoke was detected in the cabin after take-off. In 2021, an international flight with the vice president aboard had to return to Andrews following in-flight equipment failure.

The 89th AW also has a major commitment for transportation to and inside conflict zones. While many of these missions are carried out using the 89th's smaller twin-jet aircraft, at the height of the US commitment to Operation Inherent Resolve in 2014, the Department of Defense estimated that a quarter of all C-32A trips were to the US Central Command (CENTCOM) area of responsibility (AOR).

The 2021 international air evacuation in Afghanistan included extensive participation by personnel and aircraft from the 89th.

Describing the role of the 89th's personnel, US Air Force Brigadier General Stephen Snelson, CENTCOM's deputy director of operations said: "In between those CENTCOM meetings he [General Frank McKenzie, the commanding general] had calls with the [Secretary of Defense] and the [President of the United States]. Behind each of those calls was a young [communication systems operator] keeping the most important military leader in the world at that moment connected with the National Command Authority. There were flight attendants taking care of the entire team, including General McKenzie, so he could refuel and mentally be ready for his next no-fail engagement. There were pilots providing a stable platform keeping the principal on time for the next strategic meeting. Ravens protecting the aircraft and what had to be delivered in far-flung locations. Not to mention our [flying crew chiefs] who ensured that the jet stayed [mission capable] keeping that leader moving without fail."

Replacement?

Under current planning, the US Air Force will keep the C-32A in service until about 2040. In the FY2022 budget request, the US Air Force stated that it did not intend to modernise them "beyond planned modifications".

In 2018, the service issued two requests for information to industry, looking for a single type that might replace not only the C-32A but also other long-serving strategic »

A C-32A receives fuel during a stop at RAF Mildenhall, England, on February 26, 2019.
US AIR FORCE/AIRMAN 1ST CLASS BRANDON ESAU

The C-32B is the only variant of the Boeing 757 family with aerial refuelling capability.
US AIR FORCE

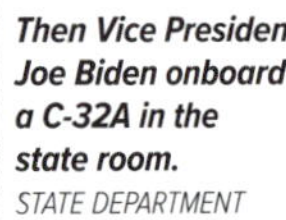

Then Vice President Joe Biden onboard a C-32A in the state room.
STATE DEPARTMENT

communications platforms: the Boeing E-4B National Airborne Operations Center (NAOC) a 747-200 airframe that accompanies *Air Force One* on some international presidential trips and the US Navy's Boeing E-6B Mercury, a 707 airframe with capabilities including strategic communications with submarines dubbed TACAMO (Take Charge And Move Out). Having a single type of aircraft – such as a modified twin-engine business jet as offered by Gulfstream or Boeing - with a designed-in capability for extensive mission-tailored communications suites appeared to offer a way forward. However, an analysis of alternatives study completed in 2020, and a US Navy requirement for a four-engine aircraft for the TACAMO mission showed that a single aircraft could not replace all three types. Consequently, in 2021, the US Air Force reallocated $6m in FY2018 funding, intended to study a C-32A replacement, to research for supersonic transport designs with the potential to provide a replacement design by 2040.

C-32B

Much has been written about the C-32B online. Real or suspected C-32B appearances on flight tracking websites are watched with great interest. Some of what has appeared on the internet about the C-32B may even be true. If the C-32A, resplendent in its attention-getting colour scheme, is the bright face of US airpower, intended for popular consumption, then the C-32B is its direct opposite, unmarked except for changing black serial numbers on a vanilla-white exterior and flying missions that are not discussed.

The US Air Force originally procured two former airline 757-200s modified by Raytheon E-Systems in Garland Texas as C-32Bs, with serial numbers 00-9001 and 02-4452.

Unlike the C-32A model, the C-32B model is powered by Rolls-Royce RB211 engines. How many C-32Bs the US Air Force is currently operating is uncertain, with estimates ranging from the official number of two to six or more.

Like the C-32A, the C-32B is linked to a particular base, squadron, and mission. While C-32As are operated by Air Mobility Command, C-32Bs are operated by Air Force Special Operations Command. The two (at least) C-32Bs were (and at least one still is) operated by the 150th

Special Operations Squadron (SOS), previously designated the 227th Special Operations Flight. This is a New Jersey Air National Guard unit, based at Joint Base McGuire-Dix-Lakehurst, New Jersey. One or more C-32Bs have also been reportedly operated by the 486th Flight Test Squadron, a US Special Operations Command unit based at Eglin Air Force Base, Florida. It's plausible that the 486th may have a flight test task, but the squadron's title is probably intended to mislead.

The 150th SOS is tasked with the Gate Keeper mission, deploying with a Foreign Emergency Support Team or FEST, a worldwide and domestic interagency rapid response force organised by the Department of State using whole-of-government capabilities.

A FEST was deployed on a C-32B to Beirut in the immediate aftermath of the devastating harbour explosion in 2020. Such teams may also deploy by C-32B for domestic contingencies. The 486th may use C-32Bs to provide similar rapid-deployment capabilities for SOCOM.

The C-32B is capable of aerial refuelling fitted with a dorsal receptacle added aft of the cockpit, using the standard US Air Force flying boom.

An internal airstair allows passenger access even to airfields that may not have equipment, as does an on-board cargo winch. The main cabin has 48 airline seats, with cargo carried in the rear of the main cabin.

A small lower cargo hold contains maintenance supplies. Internal long-range fuel tanks, originally developed by Boeing for the cancelled 757-200ER model, are fitted in the after cargo hold under a reinforced main deck; they enable an estimated 6,000nm (11,000km) range. Improved communications include satellite

Then Vice President Joe Biden in discussion with some of his staff. STATE DEPARTMENT

communications (with one or two dorsal radomes). Avionics upgrades by the Big Safari office funded in FY2016 included heads-up displays.

Unlike the C-32As, C-32Bs are not fitted with winglets.

COCO and GOCO

Contractor owned and operated (COCO) and government owned and contractor operated (GOCO) aircraft have always supplemented US airpower, the use of which has increased over the past two decades.

One reason that the number of C-32Bs in operation is uncertain is that, externally, they are difficult to distinguish from COCO and GOCO 757-200s, some of which are also fitted with dorsal SATCOM radomes.

Many COCO and GOCO 757s have an all-white colour scheme, some with only a small corporate logo or national flag marking and they change registration numbers frequently. One of the better-known COCO 757 missions is to move personnel and equipment between classified testing sites in the United States. Unconfirmed reports have also associated these aircraft with transporting terrorist suspects and prisoners.

Testbeds

The 757's contribution to US and allied airpower has certainly not been limited to the C-32 series; 757s – mainly former airliners – have been used as testbeds for new technologies. The 757's performance, size, and power generation allows it to host extensive test equipment. Its cabin has space to accommodate systems, flight test engineers, and other personnel. Industry-operated, US National Aeronautics and Space Administration (NASA), COCO and GOCO 757 testbeds have operated since the 1990s, some taking part in military training and exercises.

The best-known 757 testbed has been the Catfish (see pages 74-79), which was used to test systems for the Lockheed Martin F-22 Raptor stealth fighter. Modified from Boeing's own 757-200 prototype (N757A c/n 22212), its name comes from the F-22 wing sections mounted above the flight deck, which contain conformal radar antennas for advanced radar trials. The wing sections were thought to resemble barbels of the catfish.

The Catfish was configured with an F-22 nose and made its first flight in this configuration on March 11, 1999 and continued until 2017. During its flight-test career, the Catfish regularly operated from Edwards Air Force Base, California, Nellis Air Force Base, Nevada, Boeing Field, Seattle and St Louis-Lambert Field, Missouri.

In Uruguay with Hilary Clinton onboard. STATE DEPARTMENT/VINCE ALONG

Military 757s

Less than 20 Boeing 757s have been used by air forces or governments. While the United States has the largest fleet, it was not the first to adopt the aircraft as a VIP transport. **David Willis** reviews the role the Boeing 757 has played in military service.

The US Air Force operates the largest fleet of military Boeing 757s. In addition to the C-32As flown by the 89th Airlift Wing, responsible for VIP transport, two all-white Boeing 757-023As provide a very different transport capability. On November 7, 2002, the Mission Design Series C-32B designation was allocated to these aircraft, which are described as 'mission support aircraft used to meet transportation requirements of government agencies'. The aircraft are part of a special access programme known as Gate Keeper.

They were acquired in 2001 in a $145m contract to provide transportation for the US State Department's Foreign Emergency Support Team (FEST). According to the department, FEST "advise, assist, assess and coordinate US government crisis response activities." The lead agency for FEST is Diplomatic Security, although other interagency elements include the Department of Defense, Federal Bureau of Investigation, and the US intelligence community. Incidents in the United States – including those involving nuclear, biological, and chemical threats – are handled by the Domestic Emergency Support Team, which includes staff of the Federal Emergency Management Agency.

Unlike the C-32As, the C-32Bs are powered by Rolls-Royce RB211 engines. Additional fuel tanks are reported to have been installed in the cargo holds under the main deck, increasing range to 6,000nm (11,112km), with any cargo (limited in size by the lack of cargo doors) accommodated in the rear of the cabin. Range is further increased by the addition of a Universal Aerial Refueling Receptacle Slipway Installation, making the pair the only Boeing 757 airframes compatible with the US Air Force's flying boom-equipped tankers. Additional systems include satellite communications, which were installed in 2014 from commercial off-the-shelf units to more secure equipment, while it is understood a datalink system was added at the same time, resulting in an additional fairing on top of the rear fuselage. Work may have been undertaken by the US Air Force's Big Safari programme office, which is understood to be responsible for the overhaul of the aircraft. Big Safari undertakes high priority, rapid, limited (in terms of number of platforms) modifications of a sensitive nature that require continuing unique logistical support.

The cabins are configured for 45 passengers, with access via airstairs. Notably, photography of the exterior is not prohibited, but that of the interior of the aircraft is restricted to when they are at their home bases. When deployed overseas two aircrew must remain armed at all times.

The C-32Bs are currently operated by the 150th Special Operations Squadron (previously known as the 227th Special Operations Flight), a New Jersey Air National Guard unit based at Joint Base McGuire-Dix-Lakehurst, and the 486th Flight Test Squadron at Eglin Air Force Base, Florida. Little information

has been released about either unit, although intriguingly the 486th has the motto 'Non semper ea sunt quae videntur', attributed to the Roman 1st century fabulist Gaius Julius Phaedrus. It translates as 'Things are not always what they seem', which is true for the unit's designation as a flight test unit. It previously operated the sole Boeing C-22C (retired in December 2000) and at least one Boeing 707 (with -327C 86005 noted at Mildenhall in December 1997, plus possibly 86008) in anonymous white schemes.

White 757s

The serials of the Boeing 707s are like that seen on the first all-white Boeing 757. On February 26, 2000, a 757 lacking national insignia or unit markings, but carrying the serial 86006, was noted at Ramstein Air Base in Germany. The aircraft (N757AV, c/n 25493) had officially been leased to the US government by Asnet Inc two days earlier. It was returned to Asnet on July 10 and sold the same day to Kodiak Associates, which re-registered it as N84WA in August 2002. The aircraft passed to the US Air Force in February 2004, reportedly becoming 02-4452.

The second C-32B (c/n 25494) was originally built for Ansett Worldwide Aviation Services as N987AN for lease to Avianca, serving with the Colombian airline from April 1994 until the end of October 2000. Ansett sold it to Raytheon E-Systems, acting on behalf of the US Air Force, the following month, and the aircraft is believed to have become 00-9001.

While the airframes of both C-32Bs have been positively identified, the same cannot be said about their

military markings, as several other all-white US Air Force Boeing 757s have been noted over the years in addition to 24452 and 09001. They include 25001 recorded in late 2001, late 2005, September 2010, April 2013, January 2014, and April 2015; 96143 in late 2004, October 2009, June to September 2010, September and October 2012, April and June 2013 and September 2014, and even 86006, which made a reappearance at Tel Aviv in Israel in May 2015. The majority – if not all – are believed to be used by the two C-32Bs to disguise their real (or possibly false!) military identities.

Other White 757s

The C-32Bs are not the only all-white US 757s. A pair of aircraft are operated by the Comco Corporation, a subsidiary of L3Harris. Boeing 757-23A N226G (c/n 25491 ex N38383) and 757-22L N610G (c/n 29304 ex N1018N), delivered in January 2003 and January 2002, are believed to operate on behalf of the US Department of Defense. Exactly what role they undertake has not been disclosed, but it has been speculated that they may have worn some of the spurious military identities associated with the C-32Bs.

The US Department of Justice also operates a pair of all-white Boeing 757s. They display an American flag on the tail and differ externally from the C-32Bs and Comco aircraft by having winglets. Both are understood to be used in the Justice Prisoner and Alien Transportation System (JPATS) – more famously known as Con Air – and have been noted at various smaller US airports

loading chained prisoners overseen by armed guards. JPATS primarily moves convicts around the American prison system, but also provides support to military and state law enforcement as required. The two aircraft are 757-223s N119NA (c/n 24487) and N874TW (c/n 24524), which were delivered from L-3 Advanced Aviation in March and February 2015. Both aircraft are understood to have been modified for their role at Greenville-Majors Field, Texas – possibly under a programme overseen by Big Safari, which controls the 645th Aeronautical Systems Squadron at the airfield – and are based at Richmond International Airport, Virginia.

VIP Transports

The first country to adopt the Boeing 757 as a head-of-state transport was Mexico. Boeing 757-225 c/n 22690 was built for Eastern Air Lines as N526EA. It was rolled out on October 4, 1987, and first flew on November 2. Two weeks later it was delivered to Mexico, as TP-01 (XC-CBD) named *Presidente Carranza* with the Coordinación General de Transportes Aéreos Presidenciales (General Coordination of Presidential Air Transport, CGTAP) of the Fuerza Aérea Mexicana (Mexican Air Force). It was flown to Dallas-Love Field, Texas, for outfitting by Associated Air Center, a process that took nearly two years. At some point in 1991 its registration became XC-UJM and name *Presidente* »

The two US Air Force C-32Bs are among the most secretive aircraft operated by the service. They are the only Boeing 757s equipped for inflight refuelling. *BOEING*

Juarez, while in September 1993 it became a 757-200EM.

The aircraft was retrofitted with winglets around mid-2009 and had been repainted by mid-2013. The original fin stripes on the rudder were replaced by the Mexican national colours of green, white, and red over the whole of the tail, down to the cheatline on the rear fuselage, with a large representation of the country's seal portrayed on the fin.

With the delivery of Boeing 787 Dreamliner TP-01/XC-MEX (c/n 40695) to CGTAP on February 3, 2016, the Boeing 757 became TP-02, although it retained the same civilian callsign. Although the Dreamliner was used for many of the higher profile flights, the Boeing 757 remained in service until September 27, 2018, when it completed its last official trip, between New York-John F Kennedy Airport and Mexico City. As part of a shakeup of the Mexican government aircraft fleet, the Boeing 757 VIP transport was put up for sale, but failed to attract a buyer until August 30, 2021, when it became N226CJ. It was ferried from Mexico City to John C Munro Hamilton International Airport in Ontario, Canada, on October 27, where it was prepared for service with Cargojet Airways as C-GAJU.

Brunei and Kazakhstan

The second country to adopt the Boeing 757 as a VIP transport was Brunei, although it only used the type in the role briefly. Boeing 757-2M6 c/n 23454 was delivered to Royal Brunei Airlines on July 29, 1986, following test flights with the manufacturer as N6067U from June 11. It remained with the Brunei flag carrier for just under 18 months, as on December 5, 1987, it was transferred to the Sultan of Brunei as V8-HB1. The Boeing 757 rejoined the state airline as V8-RBC in September 1989.

The aircraft later became the only Boeing 757 to serve with two governments. On October 18, 1995, it was sold to Kazakhstan Airlines, but although the registration UN-002 was reserved it was not adopted, as the aircraft was sold to Air Finance Ltd on November 22, 1995, as VR-CRK. On the same day, it was leased to the Kazakhstan government, going to Palm Beach, California, for maintenance before entering service. The aircraft was ferried to Almaty International Airport in Kazakhstan on March 26, 1996, and the following month became P4-NSN. For a year from December 1997 the aircraft was operated on behalf of Kazakhstan by Orient Eagle Airways, before it was sold by Air Finance to Berkut Air in May 2002, becoming UN-B5701, although it continued to be used by the Kazakhstan government. By September 2019 the aircraft was noted wearing Kazakhstan Air Force titles on its fuselage.

Tango 01

Argentina used a Boeing 757 as its presidential transport for 20 years.

Boeing 757-23A T-01 (c/n 25487) first flew on July 2, 1992, having rolled-out of Boeing's Renton facility in Seattle on June 9. It was formally delivered to Ansett Worldwide Aviation Services on July 22 and immediately passed to the government of Argentina for the Fuerza Aérea Argentina (Argentine

This 'white' Boeing 757 is understood to have later become one of the two C-32B currently in service with the US Air Force. Externally, the aircraft differ little from standard 757s. KEY ARCHIVE

Air Force). Outfitting of the aircraft was undertaken at Dallas-Love Field, after which it entered service with the Ecuadrón de Avíones Presidenciales (Presidential Air Squadron) based at Aeroparque Jorge Newbery, part of Ia Brigada Aérea (Air Brigade) which had headquarters at BAM El Palomar in Buenos Aires.

The aircraft was named *Virgen de Luján* after Argentina's patron saint but became known as 'Tango 01' in service, because of its T-01 markings, previously worn by the Boeing 707-320C that the 757 replaced in 1995. For much of its career the aircraft was the subject of controversy, as it was viewed as an unnecessary and expensive perk to be abused by presidents and their closest political associates. Understandably, these complaints increased as Argentina's economic situation waned in the 1990s and early 2000s. The aircraft was also involved in several incidents in service.

On April 1, 1998, the Boeing 757 performed an aborted landing at Wellington during a state visit by President Carlos Menem to New Zealand. Strong crosswinds at the airport caused the aircraft to touch down hard before lifting off again, the pilot electing to divert to Auckland. One of the Rolls-Royce RB211 engines caught fire soon after taking-off from Aeroparque Jorge Newbery on October 1, 2004. The pilots managed to make a successful landing at nearby El Palomar and the fire was extinguished, after which the engines went to Israel for repair and overhaul, permitting T-01 to return to service in mid-2005. Presidential use of the 757 decreased markedly after the incident, however, President Néstor Carlos Kircher continued to charter Boeing 747s from Aerolíneas Argentina for his oversea visits once the 757 was unavailable. He remained in power into December 2007.

Boeing 757 '86006' was the first US 'white 757' noted, appearing at Ramstein AB in Germany in February 2000. KEY ARCHIVE

Boeing 757-200EM XC-UJM was operated by the Coordinación General de Transportes Aéreos Presidenciales of the Fuerza Aérea Mexicana and named Presidente Juarez. AIRTEAMIMAGES/STEVE FLINT

His successor – and wife – President Cristina Elisabet Fernández de Kirchner did fly in T-01. She was onboard the 757 on April 19, 2009, when the cockpit windscreen cracked, resulting in an emergency landing at Simón Bolívar International Airport in Bolivia.

Storage and Replacement

Soon after entering office in December 2015, President Mauricio Macri requested a review of the Agrupación Aérea Presidencial (Presidential Air Group), which resulted in its disbandment in 2016. The Boeing 757 was placed into storage at El Palomar and its certificate of airworthiness expired in mid-2016.

In 2020 the administration of President Alberto Fernández announced its intention to return Tango 01 to service, although work was delayed by the COVID-19 pandemic. Overhaul of the aircraft was to be undertaken in co-operation with FADEA of Córdoba, with modifications including installing additional fuel tanks to increase range to 5,500nm (10,200km). After corrosion was found on the fuselage and in the engines, options were explored to either repair or replace the aircraft. Argentina worked with the International Civil Aviation Organisation, a United Nations organisation, to find a replacement.

In August 2002, C-32B 02-4452 was registered as N84WA (c/n 25493) and passed to the US Air Force in February 2004. AIRTEAMIMAGES/ RALF MAYERMANN

On May 24, 2022, Argentina reviewed a proposal from C&L Aviation Group of Bangor, Maine, for a 2000-vintage Boeing 757-256, already equipped with the additional fuel tanks and winglets. In April 2023, a £22.23m deal was signed for the aircraft.

Royal Health Care

One of the more specialised roles undertaken by a government-owned Boeing 757 is that of mobile hospital.

Boeing 757-23A N226G (c/n 25491 ex N38383) is operated by the Comco Corporation, a subsidiary of L3Harris. It is believed to operate on behalf of the US Department of Defense.
JIM WINCHESTER

A single aircraft, Boeing 757-23A c/n 25495, was created for the Saudi royal family. Rolled out on January 10, 1994, and first flown 17 days later as N1786B, the green airframe was delivered to Ansett Worldwide Aviation Services in June 1994 as N275AW, going to Marana in Arizona that September for temporary storage. By the end of the year, it was being painted at Dothan Regional Airport in Alabama and on March 23, 1995,

was registered HZ-HMED, arriving at Riyadh two days later. Conversion as a mobile hospital was undertaken at Dallas-Love Field from August 1995, after which the aircraft returned to Riyadh in March 1997, painted with Saudi Arabian titles. In service, the aircraft provides medical support to the extended Saudi royal family, The duty had previously been undertaken by a modified Lockheed C-130H Hercules.

Fleet
Disposition

Just under half of the Boeing 757s built remain in service, 40 years after the type's maiden flight, and 17 years after the last example was delivered. **Jon Lake** outlines the in-service fleet's disposition.

Boeing built just over a thousand examples of the Model 757. N757A, the prototype, was followed by 913 757-200 airliners, 80 757-200APF freighters, a single Combi 757-200M and 55 stretched 757-300 passenger airliners. Just under half of these 1,050 Boeing Model 757s remain in service, 40 years after the type's maiden flight, and 17 years after the last example was delivered. Moreover, unlike other geriatric airliners, the 757 has not been relegated to solely hauling freight, nor to serving only second-rate airlines in forgotten corners of the world. About one quarter of the survivors still fly in the colours of two of America's major carriers – Delta and United – and it was only the COVID-19 pandemic that resulted in the type's withdrawal by American Airlines itself! Prior to that, American Airlines had operated the largest 757 fleet, with 142 aircraft in service, some of them acquired from TWA.

And yet, although the 757 had initially found great success, sales dried up during the late 1990s. The development of the stretched-fuselage 757-300 was not enough to arrest the decline, and just 55 aircraft were built – hardly enough to justify the cost of developing the new variant.

Thoughts of another, re-engined 757 derivative were abandoned in favour of a Boeing middle of the market (MOM) airliner, which subsequently became the NMA (New Midsize Aircraft) and then (very provisionally) the 797, before development was cancelled in favour of a programme to resolve the 737 MAX crisis.

There is no obvious candidate engine for a new 757-sized aircraft (the existing RB211-535 is a 43,000lb class engine) – while any such aircraft would also need a new, higher aspect ratio, lower drag wing if it were to compete with aircraft like the A321XLR.

Boeing was thereby forced to cease production, and the 1,050th and last 757 was rolled off the Renton production line on October 28, 2004, and it was delivered to Shanghai Airlines in April 2005 after several months in storage.

Longevity

What, then, accounts for the extraordinary longevity of the Model 757?

What has always set the 757 apart from other narrow bodied, single aisle airliners is its performance – thanks largely to its relatively high thrust-to-weight ratio, and to its robust four-bogie main undercarriage. This allows the 757 to operate from shorter runways, and from hot, dry, or high-altitude airports such as Albuquerque, Denver, Las Vegas, and Phoenix. In the 1980s, some even dubbed the 757 the Atari Ferrari because of its then state-of-the-art glass cockpit and excellent performance.

This feature was not some lucky accident – the 757 was designed specifically to give airlines an aircraft that would allow them to provide added capacity to high-frequency, short- and medium-haul shuttle services in the US, and this always entailed being able to operate in and out of smaller airports. The 757 provided an aircraft that airlines could use to manage seasonal shifts in passenger traffic, allowing a route to be operated profitably even if demand fell, making larger-capacity wide-bodied aircraft unprofitable.

Although it was designed as a replacement for the 727, the 757 piggy-backed on the development of the larger 767, whose development had started earlier. The two aircraft have a common cockpit, and systems that are designed to allow a common set of flight crew operating procedures to be used. This saved time and cost, and allowed a common type rating for pilots, making the 757 more attractive than other narrow bodies.

Interestingly, the 757 produces such powerful wingtip vortices (in some cases more powerful than those of a 767 or 747), that the relatively tiny 757 is classified as heavy by air traffic controllers helping them to ensure sufficient spacing behind a 757 in the pattern.

The big three US major airlines (American Airlines, Delta Air Lines and United Airlines) initially used the 757 primarily on high-density domestic trunk routes, while one of the launch customers, British Airways, profitably operated the aircraft on its own high density short routes including London to Manchester (150 miles) and London to Edinburgh and Glasgow (350 miles).

The Boeing 757's relatively long range and ETOPS certification has also allowed it to operate 'thinner' transatlantic services – on those routes between US East Coast hubs and secondary European destinations, where passenger volumes are insufficient to allow profitable operation by higher capacity wide body airliners. Flying in the opposite direction, several European operators have used the type to operate services to secondary US East Coast destinations and on seasonal services to the Caribbean.

The 757's performance, range and economic characteristics made it a firm favourite with holiday/charter airlines. At its peak, more than 70 examples of the type served with UK operators Astraeus, First Choice Airways, Monarch Airlines, Thomas Cook Airlines, Thomsonfly, Titan Airways, and XL Airways, serving European, transatlantic, and intercontinental destinations.

Until very recently, it was difficult to find an adequate narrow-body, single aisle replacement for a 757, and as an interim step, several operators simply modernised and upgraded their 757s! One early modification was the addition of winglets to reduce drag and thereby reduce fuel burn and increase range. This had the additional benefit of reducing the 757's formidable wingtip vortices!

The first winglet was designed by Aviation Partners Boeing (APB) whose Blended Winglets were originally developed in the late 1990s for the 737NG. Aircraft equipped with these were redesignated as the 757-200W or 757-200WL. The new winglets increased range from 3,915nm (7,250km) to 4,100nm (7,600km).

In 2013, APB introduced a new Scimitar Blended Winglet (SBW) to the 757. The new design replaced the Blended Winglet's aluminium cap with a sharply swept-back tip and added an aerodynamic trailing-edge wedge to the lower part of the winglet. The SBW reduced fuel burn by a further 1.1% (6% by comparison to a 757 without winglets). Icelandair and United have retrofitted their 757s with the scimitar tipped winglets.

Before their retirement, many American Airlines' 757s gained an all-business class cabin with lie-flat seats and Wi-Fi connectivity, while both Delta and United have installed new slimline seats on their aircraft. Icelandair went further, adding new seats and Global Eagle Entertainment »

Astraeus 757-200 G-STRX (c/n 25621) wearing Iron Maiden titles to denote its tasking in support of the English heavy metal band's 2011 world tour. The aircraft is seen at Santiago, Chile.
AIRTEAMIMAGES/ANDRES CONTADOR

satcom systems offering gate-to-gate Wi-Fi, with LED lighting throughout the cabin.

Boeing's troubled 737 MAX 10 offered formidable efficiency and cost effectiveness and comes close to offering the same capacity and range (ten seats fewer and 100 miles less reach) but cannot provide the hot and high or short-field performance of the 757. This should not, perhaps, be all that surprising.

The 737 MAX is based on a scaled-up regional design, and as such is considerably lighter and cheaper than a 757, following what some have called a 'Walmart kind of philosophy, the cheapest thing that only-just-fits the requirements…'

Boeing briefly considered its unbuilt 787-3 and the 767X or the Boeing 757 Plus as replacements for today's 757 fleet but may have 'missed the boat' with the emergence of Airbus' A321 Neo and A321XLR – and with the putative A322 (an A321 lengthened by four passenger seat-rows, with a new wing) waiting in the wings.

The Airbus A321LR and XLR, the long-range versions of the A321neo, already use 25% less fuel than the 757, and American Airlines has now ordered a total of 50 A321XLRs as 757 replacements, while on December 3, 2019 United Airlines announced

an order to purchase 50 new Airbus A321XLR aircraft to replace its Boeing 757-200 fleet, with deliveries due to begin in 2024.

Retirement of the 757 fleet is starting to gather pace. Some 625 Boeing 757 aircraft remained in service in December 2020, but by December 2024, just 525 were active, with another 50 or so parked. Airframes in freighter configuration and military/government use still number about 200..

Surviving Airliners

The largest operator of the 757 airliner is Delta Air Lines, who still has some 88 active Boeing 757-231s, -232s, -251s, -2Q8s, and -26Ds, and 15 757-351s in use, many of them equipped with winglets. The original Delta variant was the 757-232, while the 757-231s originally came from TWA, the -251s and -351s from Northwest, the -2Q8s from TWA, and the -26Ds originally from Shanghai Airlines. In late 2019,

Wayne Gilbert West, Delta's chief operating officer and senior executive vice president said that although "we've retired some 757s already and we've got retirement plans" because "the delivery cycles of our 757s were staggered... a large portion of those retirements are out in the more distant horizon."

United Airlines still operates around 40 757-224s and about 21 -324s and -33Ns. All were ex-Continental Airways aircraft, though the -33Ns were originally delivered to American Transair. United has 21 B757-300s, including inactive aircraft, and as such has more of the stretched version than Delta, Condor, Icelandair, and Azur Air Ukraine. United reconfigured its -300s in 2018, increasing the number of seats to 234 and making it even more competitive, reducing cost per seat mile while increasing revenue capability per flight. The stretched aircraft operate mainly to Chicago O'Hare, Denver, Los Angeles, and San Francisco.

With 11 Boeing 757-200s active, together with one 757F, and one 757APF and a pair of 757-300s, Icelandair is another major operator of the type. One of the 757-200s is the Þingvellir (pronounced Thingvellir) Sovereignty Aircraft, the newest member of the carrier's special livery family. Decorated in the blue, white and red of the Icelandic flag, the aircraft celebrated the 100th anniversary of Icelandic National Sovereignty in 2018.

German charter operator Condor was the launch customer for the stretched Boeing 757-300, with an order for 12 being announced at the Farnborough Airshow in September 1996. Because of development and cost concerns, some planned upgrades were not implemented (including an advanced cockpit taken from the Next Generation 737) but the stretched variant did receive enhanced avionics, upgraded engines, and a redesigned interior; it remains the longest single-aisle twinjet aircraft ever built. The new version entered service with Condor on March 19, 1999.

Condor operates the type with two slightly different interiors, one with 26 Premium Economy Class seats and 239 economy class seats, the other with 36 business class seats and 224 in economy. The version with 265 seats is used for Condor's short-haul and medium-haul flights to the most popular holiday destinations within Europe and to North Africa, while the 260-seat version is also used for longer routes – including for charter flights to Dubai.

Eight of Condor's 13 stretched 757-330WLs remain active, though they are expected to be retired by 2028. Two of the aircraft have been painted in Condor's new 'striped' livery, with concentric rings along the length of >>

Before Donald Trump was elected President of the United States, the tycoon used 757-200 N757AF (c/n 25155) as his personal jet. The aircraft is seen at Paris Charles de Gaulle. AIRTEAMIMAGES/ JONATHAN ZANINGER

the fuselage and vertical stripes on the tailfin.

D-ABOB wears a so-called Passion scheme, with red and white stripes, while D-ABOI's Sea scheme is based on blue and white stripes.

The next biggest 757 airline operator is Russia's Azur Air, which currently operates seven of the 10 Boeing 757-200s that it has on charge. Sunday Airlines of Kazakhstan have three Boeing 757-200s, operated by SCAT Airlines.

Other operators of the passenger carrying 757 have much smaller fleets, New Pacific Airways and Turkmenistan Airlines each have three 757-200s, while Azur Air Ukraine has three 757-300s. The Turkmen and NPA aircraft are parked.

Several airlines and operators have recently flown a single or pair of 757s, many of which are now largely parked or retired. These include Azerbaijan Airlines, Titan Airways, Uzbekistan Airways, GainJet Aviation (Greece), Jet Magic (Malta), MLW Aviation (Dallas, USA), Privilege Style (Spain), Tajik Air, and Cabo Verde Airlines.

Some of the charter 757s lead interesting lives. Jet Magic's 9H-AVM supported the 2019 Joshua Tree Tour by Irish rock band U-2. Astraeus (which ceased trading in 2011) provided a 757 for tours by a band fronted by one of its own pilots – since Iron Maiden lead singer Bruce Dickinson was a qualified commercial pilot with the carrier. Two separate aircraft became the so called *Ed Force One*: firstly G-OJIB in 2008/2009, and then G-STRX in 2011.

Private Jets

Other 757s have become luxurious private jets.

N757AG, described in a sales brochure as "one of the rare gems in luxury private aviation today". The aircraft was fitted with just 39 seats, with up to 21 fully lie-flat beds, a master bedroom, lounges, a guest room, office, and a shower. LED lighting was provided throughout, audio-visual systems, including large-format TVs and surround sound, wireless internet connectivity and a galley.

Another 757-200, N757AF, was used by Microsoft boss Paul Allen before being sold to the Trump organisation. The aircraft replaced a VIP-configured Model 727 and was famously used as Trump Force One during his presidential campaign. The aircraft was placed in storage during Trump's Presidential term but has now been restored.

Freighters

But today's 757s increasingly make their livings as freighters. The biggest operator of the 757 freighter is the package and parcel giant, FedEx Express, whose fleet still includes 92 Boeing 757-200Fs, with nine more leased to Canada's Morningstar Air Express. All wear the Fedex white and purple livery.

UPS Airlines adds a further 75 Boeing 757-200PFs to the global freighter fleet tally, while several carriers working for DHL, and wearing that company's striking yellow and red livery, account for 32 more.

DHL Aero Expreso based in Panama has three of these, while DHL Air Austria operates 17 757-200Fs and a single 757-200PF. DHL Air UK has five aircraft, and European Air Transport Leipzig adds seven more Boeing 757-200Fs.

But even added together, DHL narrowly fails to grab the third spot in the list of 757 freighter operators by size. That honour instead goes to China's SF Airlines which has 40 Boeing 757-200PCFs

on charge, with three more expected to join the fleet.

China is something of a Mecca for any avid 757 enthusiast, since YTO Cargo Airlines still operates ten Boeing 757-200PCFs (with one more due), and China Postal Airlines has five active Boeing 757-200PCFs. Two of North-Western Cargo's three Boeing 757-200Fs remain active, while one of Air China Cargo's four Boeing 757-200PCFs may still be active, though the remainder are parked, as are China Air Cargo's pair of two Boeing 757-200PCFs.

Canada's Cargojet is another major operator, with a 16 aircraft fleet including 14 active Boeing 757-200PCFs, and two parked. Amerijet International and India's Blue Dart Aviation each operate six Boeing 757 freighters, while Russia's Aviastar-TU and Spain's Cygnus Air each have five aircraft.

Asia Pacific Airlines and Air Transport International each have four freighters, but in each case, only three are active, while Spain's Swiftair operates three and Belgium's ASL Airlines has two more. Single 757 freighters are operated by Astral Aviation of Kenya, E-Cargo in Russia, Georgia's Geo-Sky, and MIAT Mongolian Airlines.

Several government and military operators have used 757s for strategic airlift and VIP transport. Details can be found in respective sections of this edition.

Though fleet size is now dwindling, we can expect to see the 757 flying for several more years to come, and we may even be able to celebrate the type's 50th anniversary in 2032! ✈